GUIDO'S CREDOS

The Paisan Point of View on Everything from Marriage to Macaroni

Vinnie Penn

CAMBRIDGE HOUSE PRESS
NEW YORK § TORONTO

Published by
Cambridge House Press
New York, NY 10001
www.camhousepress.com

Library of Congress Cataloging-in-Publication Data

Penn, Vinnie.
  Guido's credos : the paisan point of view on everything from marriage to macaroni / by Vinnie Penn.
    p. cm.
  Includes bibliographical references and index.
  ISBN 978-0-9814536-2-0 (paper over board : alk. paper)
  1. Italian Americans--Humor. I. Title.

PN6231.I85P46 2008
818'.602--dc22

                                          2008034116

Cover design by Katie Richanbach.
Composition and typography by Rachel Trusheim.

10 9 8 7 6 5 4 3 2 1

                  Printed in the United States of America.

For my father, who would have loved this book;
and for my mother,
who would have preferred that I sold some fiction.

Soundtrack available on Picklehead Music at
www.picklehead.com

www.vinniepenn.net

Acknowledgments

Special thanks to Drew Nederpelt, Rachel Trusheim, and everyone else at Cambridge House who invited The Guido to dinner. Thanks to Rockin' Richard Mayo, Matt Bialer, and Gorman Bechard. On a personal note, thanks to the only three people in my life who understand and respect the spell writing casts over me (two of whom are under five years old): Maredoll, Stella, and Luke.

When I was a kid I worked a lot of Italian places—places like Fonzo's Knuckle Room, Aldo's, formerly Vito's, formerly Nunzio's. That was a tough one, Nunzio's. On the menu they had broken leg of lamb.

Rodney Dangerfield

Friggin' Preface

I remember the day that I finally decided to embrace my heritage. It was March 9, 2005. I was 37. An unseasonably and downright unreasonably cold morning—breaking a record even—my knuckles were as red as the rose I was clutching. I was at Saint Ann's Cemetery in Providence, Rhode Island. It was my father's funeral.

The old man succumbed to lung cancer two months into his seventieth year. Next to him, as he gave the dying of the light the finger, was me, and on his nightstand a deck of playing cards and a pack of Lucky Strikes. He reeked of nicotine, God bless him.

The father I knew embraced every Italian American stereotype possible. A portrait of Sinatra hung in our living room growing up; we had ziti every Sunday at two; he was arrested several times for booking; we had cable television illegally; *The Godfather* was *Citizen Cane* as far as he was concerned and if, fresh from some Film Theory class in college one of his four children suggested this was ridiculous, we'd be ejected from the room and Orson Wells would be deemed a "fag."

Even while I was named after him, and inasmuch as Vinnie is arguably the most predominant Italian name, I never felt that I looked or sounded overtly Italian, at least when I was a teenager, and I showed little to no interest in rectifying that. On Christmas Eve, when the entire family would be indulging in every fish dish imaginable, from calamari to zuppa di pesci, I would have pizza. This was not an act of rebellion, however; I just don't like seafood. What made matters worse, though, was that it was usually frozen pizza.

My love of frozen pizza and Spaghettios antagonized my father to no end. Dad would wince annually, hit me in the head with a wooden spoon, and look accusatorily at my mother, as if to suggest a dalliance with our soda delivery guy resulted in my birth.

As time went on I even came to see many of the things associated with Italian Americans as embarrassing, grimacing through *Goodfellas* or *Casino* while my friends cheered and looked for non-Italians to start fights with. I became quite concerned with coming off as a "cavone," which loosely translates to an Italian behaving obnoxiously; someone who basically wears his ethnicity on his sleeve in one way or another: sporting a "fanny bag" around his waist or a ring on his pinky of a lion's head wherein the eyes are rubies or, easily the worst of the lot, by loudly pronouncing "three" as "tree."

Not long after Dad was diagnosed I took him to see Al Martino in concert. Martino is probably best known as Johnny Fontane in *The Godfather*, the guy who goes to Vito Corleone on his daughter's wedding day to ask for a favor. When Martino launched into "I Have But One Heart" from the film, full orchestra in tow and enormous screen with images from the movie being projected onto it behind them all, the crowd went wild, sweat permeating their linen shirts, and I suspect the sweat to have been 80 percent Sambucca.

Interestingly, this very concert is when I first began to regret my lackluster interest in my heritage during my formative years. The music, the food—isn't that what unites a culture? The show was excellent. Martino was the consummate entertainer, adept at both hitting outrageous notes, especially for a man his age, and at telling hilarious stories that absolutely resonated with the crowd, conjuring up images of all of our kitchens, a collective kitchen as it were.

My father was suspicious when I told him how much I enjoyed the show on the ride home. Still, he relinquished his *Martino's Greatest Hits* cassette shortly thereafter, which is playing in the background as I write this ("Spanish Eyes," Track 2, Side 1).

Slowly but surely over the course of that year I inquired about certain things: relatives from Federal Hill (where he grew up in Rhode Island), or what particular words I'd overheard him say in Italian over the years translated to. I even had him teach me how to make his sauce.

But it wasn't until they began to lower him into the ground that I truly decided to immerse myself to some degree, as best as I could anyway, especially as I had just become a father myself and would want to imbue my children with their grandparents' and their grandparents' grandparents' culture. During the ride in the limousine from Connecticut, where Dad had moved to marry my mother and raise his children, and where the services were that blustery morning, I read and re-read his obituary. There were so many long, crazy Italian names on it that it looked more like a menu from a Mulberry Street eatery. Staring at me from the top was the family name, a name I had shortened significantly to Penn some 15 years earlier when my writing career began. He didn't so much mind the abbreviation as prefer I go with Penna, staunchly advocating a vowel at the end, which I repeatedly dismissed.

Graveside, the decision was made to embrace my heritage, no, to downright celebrate the stereotypes. March 9th was the day. Carpe fuckin' Diem.

CHAPTER ONE
"Getting" the Boot

> ## Guido Credo No. 1
> History: What it comes down to is your story against *his*.

What better captures a group of Italian Americans inter-acting: a scene from a Martin Scorsese film or an Olive Garden commercial?

Take your time.

The answer to that question is a time-honored one: It depends who you ask.

Consider the many who deem Scorsese's films not only excessively violent, but that the violence is glorified to boot, the Italian Americans committing the acts seemingly reveling in their malevolence. Also consider the preposterously white-bread inhabitants of those Olive Garden commercials, their buoyancy ostensibly attributed to bottomless salad bowls and all-you-can-eat breadsticks.

In both cases stereotypes run amok, and stereotypes play a pivotal part in every ethnic group's history.

According to the 2000 U.S. census, almost 16 million

Italian Americans live in the United States. Italian Americans constitute about 6 percent of the U.S. population, an alarmingly smaller percentage than you probably would have guessed. Most are grandchildren and great-grandchildren of the 3.8 million Italian-born immigrants who entered the United States from 1899 to 1924. In the years since, this number has probably risen, though not dramatically, and it could have dipped as well.

Of that 6 percent, however, the majority have definitely seen at least some of Scorsese's work, while the same number would tell you they—and I quote with confidence—"could give a fuck about all-you-can-eat breadsticks."

This is how I believe the pitch meetings go for an Olive Garden commercial:

Account Executive: We need the family to be loud so they can drown out the sound of all the can openers whirring in the kitchen. This'll work great too, as all Italian families are loud.

Client: Our main concern is the carbonara.

Account Executive: Well…we can't address the chain's ventilation issues in a commercial.

Client: Carbonara is a type of sauce you idiot! It's what we're pushing this quarter, our ziti carbonara, fettucini carbonara…

Account Executive: Oh, right, right. Of course. Well, great, have the father figure in the spot sop up the last bit of carburetor sauce…

Client: Carbonara! Carbonara sauce! How did you

get this account anyway? Do you guys do rock, paper, scissors around here or what?

Account Executive: I apologize. Anyway, have the dad sop up the last bit of sauce—Italians love to do that—with a breadstick, and then the voiceover kicks in…(overly dramatic pause)… "and don't forget the all-you-can-eat breadsticks."

The Account Executive sits back, completely pleased with himself, when the advertising agency's head probably chimes in: "No, no, say 'and the all-you-can-eat breadsticks…don't fuhgettaboutit'!!"

Laughter fills the conference room.

Now, simply put, stereotypes are not worth fighting over, or at least, most of them aren't, particularly the food associated with a specific ethnic group. Of all things! Were someone to shout at me out their car window after I've cut them off, "Hey, you with the big gold horn hanging around your neck—go eat some pasta and get off the road!" my reaction would honestly be, "Hmmm, not a bad idea. Been a while since I had some cavatelli."

Telling someone of French descent to "go eat a crepe" or a Mexican a taco or, yes, dare I say, suggesting an African American who angered you in some capacity to "eat some collard greens" is just not deserving of fisticuffs.

After all, were these—*are* these—not the foods of our youth, of our ancestors, a taste bud harbinger of memories, and wonderful ones at that? Of *course* they are.

A cookbook of Italian dishes will have page upon page of pasta dishes; French cookbooks will endeavor to explain how to prepare a variety of crepes; while there is no "recipe" for collard greens there will no doubt be a beautiful photograph of a plateful gracing the pages of an African American cookbook, albeit on a sprawling table alongside perhaps golden fried whiting fish and candied yams. Like a stick of pepperoni on the cutting board behind Giada DeLaurentiis in my copy of *Everyday Italian*. Love that picture.

Food, slang, fashion sense—indicative of our cultural backgrounds but not worth potentially winding up in the hospital. Such loosening up would do the world a world of good.

This said, some stereotyping is too offensive as to be deemed acceptable. Assuming an Italian American is a mobster just because he is an Italian American? That is simply prejudicial, insulting, and wrong. Assuming an African American is a rapper just because he is an African American? That is simply prejudicial, insulting, and wrong. Assuming a Frenchman is a coward just because he is a Frenchman? Ooh, that reminds me, I haven't spoken to my friend Pierre in a while. He changed his telephone number after getting a few crank calls.

The intent of this book is to mine the treasure trove of material that is associated with Italians, only steering clear, obviously, of the truly reprehensible (not to mention illegal). Largely, stereotypes are born of our respective histories and as such should conjure up pride.

The earliest Italian immigrants settled in New York City and San Francisco. In 1860 New York City had an Italian population of ten thousand. By 1920 almost one-fourth of all Italian immigrants lived there, while more than half lived in the middle Atlantic states and New England. They almost immediately established distinctive ethnic neighborhoods known as Little Italies, not unlike an animal marking its territory via urination.

Which food was first where is, to this day, still disputed. (Refer to Credo #1.) The debate over where the very concept of a slice of pizza was born, and served, will result in carnage in certain circles.

During the 1920s and 1930s, Italian American politicians began to win elections for (i.e. infiltrate!) public office, such as New York City mayor Fiorello La Guardia (after whom the airport is obviously named) and New York congressman Vito Marcantonio. Write-in ballots were rumored to cause carpal tunnel syndrome for many throughout the boroughs of the Bronx, Brooklyn, Queens, and Staten Island, altering stickball game results over the course of hundreds of neighborhood blocks.

Even while public office records can attest to the outstanding accomplishments of these two men and credit their respective wins as precipitous, both men are still rumored to have laid claim to things neither had anything to do with, as that is the Italian way. La Guardia was said to often infer at cocktail parties that it was his ancestors who shaped the actual landscape of Italy, deciding collectively that it should be a boot. Marcantonio, it has long been whispered in certain circles, once declared a relative to have pantsed Christopher Columbus on his own ship.

Simply put, there is an innate fondness for exaggeration and hyperbole when it comes to the Italian. Wherein a non-

Italian, in an effort to relay that something has happened several times, will say just that, *It has happened several times*, an Italian will say, "It happened 42 times."

Additionally, an Italian American has a proclivity toward claiming either ownership or invention, or at the very least "knows someone" who was involved.

Wedding Reception, Present Day: *Three couples who have never met before sit at a round table, place cards before them.*

"The ceremony was beautiful! How about the bride's gown?" gushes one female guest.

"Oh, wasn't it gorgeous? I think it was Versace," counters another female guest.

"I did shooters with Versace's landscaper once," the Italian American female guest will ultimately say, outing herself.

"I'm starving," a male guest will then interject.

"There's bread in the basket there," another male guest will inform him.

"My family's descended from the baker who came up with Italian bread," the Italian American male guest will boast, perhaps punctuating the statement with a raucous, "Descended like my balls!"

Guido Credo No. 2

Work: Do as much as you're able.
Even more if it's under the table!

The phrase "under the table" means getting paid in cash at your workplace, sans paperwork. Yes, it basically translates to tax evasion. The dishwashing jobs of my teenage years were all "under the table," but this was more due to the fact that I was not of working age yet rather than ripping off the government. There are lots of reasons why a person wouldn't want a paper trail of him or herself.

Aren't there?

Even though about 65 percent of Italian immigrants were farmers in Italy, when they first arrived in America most headed for cities where labor was needed and wages were relatively high. They worked seasonal and unskilled jobs building railroads, streets, skyscrapers, and public transportation systems; mining coal; or working in steel, shoe, and auto plants. Many of the women who followed the men to the United States found work in the urban garment trades, canneries, and textile mills. Immigrant children often left school before graduating to help their families earn money.

A phrase as popular as "under the table" in the Italian community is "fell off a truck." When someone offers you a deal on, say, a case of toilet paper, and you remark on how cheap you're getting it and then inquire as to how they can sell it so cheap, they are likely to respond that it "fell off a truck." This is meant to suggest that the truck carrying the dozens of cases of toilet paper hit an enormous bump in the road, or perhaps a pothole, and the case you're getting "fell off," with the person approaching you about it being the finder.

To take this literally would mean you are "stunato," by the way.

Nonetheless, by the middle of the last century such phrases had truly entered the lexicon. Living the American dream had not only become doable, it was every bit as wonderful as expected, and the workload necessary every bit as exhausting. But the advances were undeniable, not only in the world of politics but also in the world of entertainment.

And the "hardest working man in showbiz" was "Ol' Blue Eyes" himself, the "Chairman of the Board" (have I mentioned hyperbole yet?), Frank Sinatra.

Guido Credo No. 3
Jesus may not have been Italian, but Sinatra sure as hell was.

Sinatra might be the single most important Italian American in history. He was a singer, comedian/storyteller, heartthrob, and actor all at once, excelling at all of it, and even had a president's ear. He turned chasing tail with your buddies into an art form merely by naming it "The Rat Pack," and landed a long overdue hard right hook on the jaw of racism with its inclusion of the equally incomparable Sammy Davis Jr.

"I'm truly fortunate to be counted among Frank's friends," Dean Martin said upon opening his now-infamous "Dean Martin Celebrity Roast of Frank Sinatra." "I'm pretty lucky. Every night I get on my knees and pray. I pray that I could get off my knees."

But Sinatra's standing was truly born of hard work. While the singing may have come easy to him, the acting was a tad more elusive, making his Academy Award-winning turn in *From Here to Eternity* as sweet as a spoonful of Nutella.

Evidence of Sinatra's prominence in the acting community is also on display at the roast, in the form of no other than Jimmy Stewart and Orson Welles. In his closing comment, Welles even acknowledged Frank's heritage thusly:

"In closing, I'd like to speak as an Italian. I am an Italian the hard way, by marriage. While I can't claim to have risen to those loftier circles of high society where the bent nose and slight cauliflowering of the ear are signs of sheik, what I have learned is that, with all Italians, there are some questions it's healthier not to ask."

Had Sinatra not been Welles's own daughter's godfather the portly director could have wound up being "Citizen Needs a Cane" that evening.

In any event, Sinatra left a pair of enormous shoes to fill, and every son looks to do just that. Italian American fathers want their sons to do things their way "or else." Sinatra actually set the sentiment to music, via Paul Anka's lyrics. Let us all bow our heads and take a moment of silence for Frank Sinatra Jr.

CHAPTER TWO

In the Name of the Father, the Son, and the Stromboli Spirit

Guido Credo No. 4

Your mother and father…they're like your heart, your lung, your first time with a broad; you only get one, y'know?

"Here's a fact I don't know whether you know or not: Sicilians have black blood pumping through their hearts. If you don't believe me, you can look it up. Hundreds and hundreds of years ago the Moors conquered Sicily. And the Moors are n*****s. Way back then Sicilians were like Wops from Northern Italy; they all had blond hair and blue eyes. But then the Moors moved in there and changed the whole country. They did so much fucking with Sicilian women that they changed the whole bloodline forever. That's why blond hair and blue eyes became black hair and dark skin."

So explains Dennis Hopper's character in the Quentin Tarantino-scripted film *True Romance*, to Christopher Walken's character no less. Hopper played the father of Christian Slater's character, Clarence, who was the film's focal point. Conversely, the father/son relationships of both *The Godfather* and *A Bronx Tale* are pulverized by this one scene and the Hopper and Slater characters aren't even Italian American. Michael and Vito Corleone of *The Godfather*, played, respectively, by Al Pacino and Marlon Brando, is your standard-issue Italian American idol-worship father/son scenario, even while the father in question is a Don and has horses' heads removed in his spare time—maybe even *because* of this. *A Bronx Tale* throws a monkey wrench into that concept by having the father character—played by Robert DeNiro of all people!—be a hardworking lug who steers clear of the mob and whose son still goes for the Mafioso idol worship, in this instance played by Chazz Palminteri, who also wrote the script.

In all of the films the father is willing to die for his son, but it is Hopper whose death is the grimmest, and not because of anything other than "offending" Walken's Italian American character's sensibilities.

Hopper's pseudo history lesson caused an immediate controversy, sparked debate, and could be overheard, often verbatim, at restaurants and coffee shops across the country for months afterwards. The fact that what is at the core of what Hopper says isn't exactly inaccurate caused an uneasiness amongst the older generation of Italian Americans, the ones who would proudly relay that either they or their parents were "off the boat" while simultaneously mixing their homemade wine with orange soda. They could neither laugh it off as absurd, nor could they put up their dukes, much as some might have wanted to (and probably did), with textbooks splayed before them, sections highlighted for their reading pleasure. They could only (begrudgingly?) accept the possibility.

But by far the most amusing aspect of Tarantino's audacious dialogue is that throughout the majority of the past century Italian American children were constantly reminded of the importance to "date Italian," as, no doubt, Irish Americans were to date Irish, Polish Americans Polish and so on and so forth. Talk about blowing a hole in a theory!

It is not that the majority of our ancestors were necessarily racist, although certainly a percentage was; they were merely a reflection of the time and over the years, as the lines between class and ethnicity and gender and race began to blur, most (optimistically speaking) would accept it all with a nonplussed shrug, albeit surely reflecting on how it was for them some 40 years earlier with semi-wide-eyed disbelief. Many a vantage point was not fueled by hate at all, and certainly not a superiority, just surroundings, and moreover upbringing. It probably never even occurred to many of them that an Italian American could have simply brought, say, an Irish girl home, let the storm pass, and eventually sire a Colin or Liam DeLucia.

Interestingly, the same hand-me-down logic dictated that once married you could not leave, no matter how miserable the union eventually became. Ever. Some of the most unhappily married men and women you could ever meet were your grandparents. Lifetimes literally spent grinning, bearing, and praying for a heart attack in your sleep. The men were allowed a gumar—a "mistress"—and the women were allowed to forsake electrolysis.

Hey, I'm just reading from the rulebook here.

Growing up Italian American necessitates not only knowing where in Italy your "people" come from (in my case, my paternal grandmother Ischia, paternal grandfather Caserta, and my maternal grandparents Sorrento), and with that if you were thusly Sicilian or Napolitan or Marchegian or what have you, but also having uncles who were not blood relations nor were their names actually names. I had an Uncle Tickets, an Uncle Nuts 'n Bolts and an Uncle Linguine. Nuts n' Bolts was so called due to his being a mechanic, Linguine due to the fact that he inhaled somewhere in the vicinity of six boxes of the pasta per day, and Tickets, the trickiest name of the three, so called due to his always referring to his playing cards when gambling as "tickets." The names are generally so unoriginal as to make you suspect a larger, more significant meaning. But, alas, a Fat-Ass Freddie or Tommy Two-Toes were usually indeed a Frederick who was overweight and a Thomas with only two toes on one foot.

I will now endeavor to assist you, dear reader, in ascertaining what your nickname would be in Italian circles. It is a three-step process.

First, focus on your single most embarrassing and, yes, maybe even endearing flaw. The endearing part is not mandatory, but the embarrassing sure as hell is.

Got it?

Allow me to help: Are your teeth crooked? Do you have a big nose? Bad breath?

Perhaps being more abstract is the way to go: Are you consistently unlucky? Accident prone? Do you have a history of the people you date fucking your friends?

Once you have successfully determined your most prominent flaw, it will then be of the utmost importance to settle on one word for it, two tops. For instance, if crooked teeth is what you've decided to go with, don't get all extravagant and come up with "left and right teeth" or something like that. Keep it simple, too; although the two words "crooked teeth" won't do. So come up with something like snaggletooth or chompers. Same with big nose; go instead with schnoz or beak. Even if the two words are less syllabically than the one, go with the one. Hyphenating is a matter of taste.

Lastly, alliteration is key. Crooked teeth and your name is Charlie? Homerun, my friend. "Chompers" Charlie De-Nuzzio.

What's that? Your last name is Severino? Well, then, "Snaggletooth" Severino it is.

Bonus points if you can pull off a rhyme. A guy with a huge nose whose last name is Criscuolo who gets the nickname "Schnozzollo" Criscuolo simply cannot argue.

Of course, there are exceptions. Aside from your basic "nickname by last name abbreviation" case—as in Vitagliano becoming "Vitags" or Gagliardi becoming "Gags"—there is also a prevalence of Sonny or Cheech. The Mayor of Providence is Vincent "Buddy" Cianci Jr.

My father's nickname was "The Lob." This was derived from his decidedly anti-go-getter attitude and general ability to "lob around" all day on the couch. Again, his most universal flaw became his nom de plume of sorts.

This, obviously, results in conflicting sensations for the wives, as they are at once ecstatic that the world knows of their husband's most glaring shortcoming, yet flabbergasted that his circle of friends have turned it into a cheeky nickname that he will not only accept but even respond to at, say, a baptism, perhaps even more quickly than his own God-given name. Nothing drew my mother's ire more quickly than one of my father's ne'er-do-well buddies calling the house and gleefully asking for "The Lob."

While some nicknames are not met with open arms but moreover a gritting of the teeth and palpable disdain, they are nevertheless as much a rite of passage as anything religious, owning a page of a person's past as much as their wedding ceremony or what they gave up for Lent every spring of their life.

In fact, looking back is quite possibly the number one pastime of the Italian American senior citizen, second only to playing cards and/or bocce (lawn bowling).

Guido Credo No. 5
Memories are better than pictures, plus they can never be an Exhibit A.

The Italian is the easiest to spot at an old age home, versus any other ethnic group. He is either organizing some form of gambling or rambling about the "old country" and his or her myriad adventures in life. The former, too, is merely the assembling of an audience for the latter.

For whatever reason, the present is only a vehicle for discussing the past, and the future—mobster stereotype aside—is just not something Italian Americans seem to bank on. My paternal grandfather died when I was nine, and spent those nine whole years saying upon our goodbyes at the end of visits that it was most likely the last time I'd see him.

While the majority of memories are marinated in hyperbole, with the storyteller practically alluding to being able to fly, being bulletproof, or having turned down the opportunity to run for president of the United States, storytelling as pastime simply cannot be rivaled by Super 8 projector or, more recently, camcorder. It is essential to the Italian American existence. We pride ourselves on our ability to hold a crowd's attention, wielding pregnant pauses like taut elastics, utilizing hand gestures as if we are guiding an airplane in for a safe landing.

What follows is a standard story that an older family member would most likely relay at a family get-together, initially in its no-frills, largely accurate form, and then in its Italian American glory.

Uncle: When I was a kid I walked to school every morning and home from school every afternoon. No bus, and it wasn't right down the street either!

Nieces & Nephews (in unison): Walked? Really? Even when it rained or snowed!?

Uncle: Bad weather and all, kiddies. We didn't have snowstorms back then, either—we had *blizzards*!

Nieces & Nephews: Wow, no bus!

Uncle: Nope. And when you got bullied, there was no bus driver to break it up. You were on your own.

Nieces & Nephews: What would you do, Uncle Dominic?

Uncle: You tried to reason with them or if they were really bad, sometimes you had to stand up to them and take your lumps.

Nieces & Nephews: Ooohhh.

Now, as promised, is the Italian American version:

Uncle: When I was a bambino I walked to school every morning and home from school every afternoon. No bus, and the school was, like, *tree* thousand miles away!

Nieces & Nephews (in unison): Walked? Get the fuck outta here!! Even when it rained or snowed!?

Uncle: Abso-fuckin'-lutely. And we didn't have pussy snowstorms like you kids got nowadays—we had *blizzards*! I remember one time we got somethin' like 17 feet. We were all using our chimneys to get in an' outta da house.

Nieces & Nephews: Wow, no bus!

Uncle: Nope. And when you got bullied, there was no bus driver to break it up. You were on your own.

Nieces & Nephews: What would you do, Zio Dominic?

Uncle: You busted 'em in the head wit' a tree branch. Or you duked one of your pals your suffrito on a hard roll so he did it. My pal Nato the Annihilator once *trew* a kid clean over a car for me.

Nieces & Nephews: Ooohhh.

Therein lays more than one Italian American traits, the first and foremost being the aforementioned penchant for exaggeration. Second, the wearing of a memory (or memories, as most stories tend to include a variety of side roads and stories within a story) as if it were a badge. Third, the ability (or inability actually) to mispronounce all "th" words, yet come up with a word like "annihilator."

Sidebar:
LEARNING HOW TO CONFRONT FEAR
(Italian American-style)

This particular lesson, as most Italians will tell you, usually comes via an older sibling, especially if said sibling is more than three years your senior. There is a five-year gap between my older brother and me.

Back when I shared a bedroom with him, there was an additional set of rules to adhere to, the ones with even steeper penalties than those set in place by our parents. Besides that, the rules my parents laid down were no different than at any other house really: Clean up after yourself, no talking back, a specific time to be home and not a second later, et al. The added bonus was my being the youngest, which translated to lax enforcing of said rules.

But an older brother or sister's rules are typically much trickier, and more than a little insane.

For instance, I couldn't watch the TV in our room if he was in there, even if he had turned it on and was watching one of "his shows." If he caught me looking he would rig up a blanket to block my line of sight.

I could neither open nor close the windows on his side of the room.

It goes without saying that there was no clothes, toys, or record borrowing.

I could have none of my friends up to play in our room.

I could not play any of my records in the room, particularly Shaun Cassidy, which propelled me to bring my turntable and pretty much everything else of mine down into the basement, turning it into my de facto bedroom. (This is not uncommon in Italian American homes.)

Once these rules are mastered, an older brother or sister—possibly frustrated by the younger sibling's ability to follow them, and the willingness to—may begin a potentially life-altering practical joke phase. In my case, with my brother not in any danger of sporting a creativity badge from school, the practical jokes ranged from shooting me in the head with a dart gun while I slept to shooting me in the face with a water pistol while I slept.

This being the case, it wasn't long before my ten-year-old self began dreading bedtime.

One night, as eight o'clock passed, and then nine, and with ten fast approaching, I noticed that he was conspicuously absent from the house. He had been there for dinner, had played Warren Zevon's "Werewolves of London" repeatedly afterwards, and had locked himself in the upstairs bathroom for a good, long time right after that.

I was tired. I wanted to go to bed. But where was he? I looked everywhere. I told my mother I thought something was up but, as she was on the phone with a girlfriend, she shooed me. I had repeatedly tried to convey to her and my father that their oldest son was becoming a lunatic to no avail. They chalked his bad moods and general angst up to being 15 and what he did to me up to your standard older-brother-tor-turing-younger-brother nonsense. They joked that we were Cain and Abel. At the rate we were going, it would soon be Cain and Disabled.

It was in this instant that I realized putting off what was coming only strengthened the fear, made it worse, filling my head with scenarios, each one worse than the other.

Borrowing my sister's tape recorder, I loaded it, pressed the enormous record, play, and pause buttons simultaneously, swallowed hard enough to convince myself I may have caused tonsil abrasion, and, after turning out the bedroom light, crawled under the covers. My finger was on the pause button, perspiration equal to that of a trigger. At the slightest sound I would undo the pause, thereby catching whatever sadistic "prank" my brother had planned on tape.

There was a rustling in the closet. I hit the button just as he burst out from inside there, stocking over his head and kitchen knife in his hand, growling like a madman.

While I didn't scream, I'd be lying if I didn't admit that a bowel movement was mighty close. He pulled the stocking from his head and flipped the light on, laughing heartily, but disappointed nonetheless that I hadn't run from the room like a little girl from a haunted house.

The next morning I brandished the tape recorder in the kitchen, regaling my parents with further proof of their son's descent into madness, and watching Tommy's face go white at the same time. I had one-upped him, caught him in the act, ably demonstrated that I was not only no longer to be messed with but that a career in law just might be in my future.

After it was over and I pressed stop on the battery-operated machine, my mother exclaimed "My baby!" and began hugging me furiously, a hug loaded with pity and "I'll save you from the Boogeyman" sentimentality.

As for my father, the only time he ever laughed harder was when he was watching *Sanford & Son*.

Now, getting back to the usage of words like annihilator or anything else remotely similar. It is not the misnomer one might suspect at all, but rather evidence of how integral religion—and the Bible, in particular—was to the upbringing of the Italian.

A Guido's recall when it comes to prayer is astounding, especially when compared to his lack of recall when it comes to where he was until three in the morning *that very day*.

> # Guido Credo No. 6
> Religion: Like crime, more effective when it's organized.

Life in Italian neighborhoods in the early 1900s revolved around family and church. The Catholic Church often sponsored sports and social clubs. You shot hoops with the neighborhood priest, for Christ's sake…literally!

This is not to say that this is no longer the case, but just as surely as dinner as a family has gone the way of happenstance in most homes, thanks to two-income families and what not, religion—while still a foundation (in Italian American homes baptisms rival weddings)—is not so central, and shooting hoops with your priest, well, let's leave that one alone, huh?

Rosary beads, once the ultimate accoutrement, have been replaced by belly bracelets. A tattoo on your father's arm of the crucifix has become a tattoo on the small of your mother's back with something written in Latin—no INRI in sight—in cursive below it.

Speaking of INRI, pretty much every Italian American home of the 1970s had a massive crucifix adorning their living room wall, drilled aggressively into the horrific wood paneling, the blood on Jesus' hands and feet an almost glow-in-the-dark red.

God and Jesus were talked about like they were relatives, a father and a son who were to be called over whenever a child did something quantified as wrong. "Don't apologize to me, apologize to Jesus! Ooh, when God gets a hold of you!"

Confession was a weekly occurrence, easily replaced nowadays by some appointment television. What the world may truly need now, in fact, is *CSI: The Vatican*.

Vintage black and white films—the kinds populated by James Cagney and Humphrey Bogart—typically boasted a priest character, displayed in an everyman capacity, someone from the neighborhood who grew up on the same playground as you, and still retaining a bond with the guy who "went the wrong way." The priests were your confidants, the church a sanctuary; metaphorically speaking the priest was Superman and his church, the Fortress of Solitude. Best of all, it was a Fortress of Solitude that was open to the public, 24/7, the various crystals and portals at your disposal. Today, a church is locked up in the middle of the night tighter than Superman's mobile home.

CHAPTER THREE
The Adventures of Zuppaman

Guido Credo No. 7

The second the guys who dreamed up Superman made him bulletproof, somebody else dreamed up cement shoes.

Hero worship is an important part of adolescence. To paraphrase a popular adage, you can pick your heroes but you can't pick your family.

The three most popular heroes to young Italian Americans throughout the first half of the last century, arguably, were the neighborhood cop, the neighborhood priest, and the professional ball player. Falls from grace were at once improbable and impossible. By the time the 1900s were limping toward the millennium this had changed considerably. The majority of movies being released were about "dirty" cops, priests were the thing of scandal—and the most obscene sort of scandals imaginable—and ballplayers were toppling from the mound amidst steroid abuse.

Where are our heroes?

While the gangster/mobster had not only remained a popular offshoot of the concept throughout it all, its popularity multiplied exponentially, particularly within Italian American ideology. Here came a bonanza of unlikely candidates for hero status: Ray Liotta as Henry Hill in the film *GoodFellas*. Donnie Brasco. Tony Soprano.

It seemed that even if the character was a cop it was his temptation and the resulting humanizing that ultimately made him likable, the fact that while undercover he did get swept up in it all, did go further with the blow than he intended, actually began liking the guys he went undercover to snag in the first place was a minor detail. Unblurrable lines had become blurred.

Ask yourself: Who did you prefer in *A Bronx Tale*, Robert DeNiro's character or Chazz Palminteri's? Perhaps sitting across from Lorraine Bracco as Doctor Melfi could help you sift through that muck and mire.

As for superheroes, on the pages of comic books from the 1930s through the 1970s ethnicity could not be found, and that's only slightly changed since. Race had begun to be addressed in the seventies, and some kickass African American superheroes resulted, among them Marvel Comic's immensely popular Luke Cage (interestingly, where actor Nicolas Cage got his stage name, dropping his Italian nom de plume of Coppolla). Cage even began to run with an Asian American superhero named Danny Rand, aka Iron Fist.

Still, the majority of alter egos were decidedly safe: Peter Parker. Bruce Wayne. Clark Kent. Bruce Banner. The Justice League might as well have been called the WASP

Brigade.

How come Spiderman couldn't be Peter Spazzinelli by day? Or Bruce Wayne Bruce O'Flaherty?

My friends and I searched high and low for a hero whose heritage we shared. Especially once James Bond entered the lexicon and the Brits got to shove him down our throats.

Enter Zuppaman. The Man of Veal.

Intrepid reporter Charlie "What the Fuck Chuck" Kentaggio was assigned to cover some suspect scientific experiments in town and one night, growing hungry, got some take-out from a restaurant called Il Forno. He ordered the veal special and some zuppa di pesce. During one such experiment Charlie and his food were accidentally bombarded with both radioactive and gamma rays.

Zuppaman was born.

You may have never heard of Zuppaman, but he had a considerable run during the late seventies at Saint Bernadette's School in New Haven, Connecticut: ten issues and one "king-size annual." (I was ridiculed for my hobby and to this day I am convinced it put the official start date of me dating off at least two years, but my homemade comic books were eaten up.)

Zuppaman's archenemy, interestingly, was "Yong, Master of Martial Arts," and he teamed up in two issues with a seemingly Native-American anti-hero named "Hiawatha Smith." Indicative of the era and derivative of Marvel Comics enough to warrant a cease and desist, what had begun as a joke veered into a territory resembling real comic books. The need for a superhero with a similar upbringing and, yes, ethnicity, was rooted more deeply than I knew.

To this day Stan Lee, the creator of Marvel Comics' popular X-Men, Fantastic Four, and even The Hulk and Spider-man—among many others—has oft credited Spiderman's success to the fact that here was the first alter ego who was not only a teenager but had relatable high school troubles, i.e. not being able to get a date, edged out by cliques, bullied by Flash Thompson. Peter Parker was a neurotic train wreck who lived with his Aunt May and popped a chubby over his science homework.

This ably illustrates the reason why so many questionable Italian American characters of fiction often became lionized by the public, usually to the astonishment and even dismay of screenwriters and novelists. Mario Puzo was said to have been stunned initially by the absolute embracing of his Corleone family in the *Godfather* series. It was simple really: We recognized them.

Not unlike Denis Leary's all-too-human firefighter character in the F/X series *Rescue Me*, and the Irish American community's embracing of him, we know folks like this.

Of course, groups that have the word "defamation" embroidered onto collared shirts lay in wait for televisions programs, feature films, and even comic books where they dare to give a character a name dripping with ethnicity so as to write up petitions with words like exploitation, glorification, and perpetuating as the alternating headers. Leary's character in *Rescue Me* being an alcoholic will smack of realism to some and of stereotyping to others, specifically those salivating for such a thing.

Television's Italian Sons
A minor interlude

While *Rescue Me* can surely count among its many view-ers a large percentage of Irish Americans, so too could *The Sopranos* count among its faithful many, many Italians. Hell, *Who's the Boss?* would have never seen a second season were it not Tony Danza in the lead and he didn't play up his heri-tage in that subtle way he does. (Just a theory, but I stand by it.) Arthur "The Fonz" Fonzarooski would've gotten his ass kicked. (Another theory.)

How else to explain the surprise success of the reality show *Growing up Gotti*? Outside of the headline effect, Italian Americans could identify with the mother's antics, the bois-terous boys and their seemingly endless supply of hair prod-uct—these kids were being booked for bar appearances two states removed from Jersey and people were flocking to meet them!

Scott Baio's resurgence on television came not from an in-ternet series called "Chachi 2500 A.D." (although I still have a treatment for that in my desk), but from reality television as well. Further proof of the public's fascination with the... ahem... "overly" Italian: Another VH1 reality series, *That's Amore*, a spin-off of a reality show that is a spin-off itself, wherein an Italian who can barely speak English weeps enor-mous tears as he talks about being alone.

Baio, of course, is...or was...the anti-thesis of that. One could argue it is his history and/or notoriety as a playboy that initially lured viewers to his VH1 show and made it a hit, but with the second season's title of *Scott Baio is 46...and Preg-*

nant, I would suggest that it's his forever put-upon, totally ca-vone demeanor and Italian horn swinging from a chain on his neck that's at least keeping them there.

Speaking of which (and speaking of theories), what is *The Sopranos* if not this generation's *Happy Days*?

Bear with me.

David Chase may have buried the homage, but not six feet deep, not by a long shot. Tony Soprano is "The Fonz" and Christopher is Chachi. The relationships are identical, just without The Fonz having ever actually murdering Cha-chi (though he clearly could have and probably even wanted to on many occasions, like when Chachi accidentally burned down Arnold's).

From there Chase gets slippery, though: Uncle Junior is the Howard Cunningham figure, and Carmela is "Mrs. C" (Chase throws us a bone here), while Meadow and AJ are Joanie and Richie respectively. Silvio and Paulie Walnuts are Ralph Malph and Potsie Webber respectively. Artie is Arnold, serving up shenanigans and shellfish at the restaurant at the core of the series (one may argue it is instead "The Bada-Bing," but not much of a menu there). Jennifer Melfi is Jenny Piccolo, doling out advice that may or may not be worthwhile.

It's all pretty obvious. To me anyway.

In today's politically correct obsessed climate, Fonzie's "Sit on it" would surely draw the ire of a gay and lesbian defamation group, just as Superman himself can now seemingly only stand for "truth and justice," the "American way" part having been clipped from the 2006 film incarnation directed by Bry-an Singer and starring Brandon Routh and Kate Bosworth.

How insane is that?

FIRST TABLE READING OF SCREENPLAY FOR *SUPERMAN RETURNS*:

Lois Lane: Perry, Superman is back!

Jimmy Olsen: This is big news. I haven't felt emasculated in ages.

Perry White: Get on it you two! Find out everything… where he's been, if he still stands for truth, justice and the American way…

Trembling Studio Exec: (from beneath craft services table) We have to cut that part! You have to cut "American way"! Can we change it to "Earthly way"? It reeks of superiority and just begs for another 9/11…!

The irony seemed to be lost on all involved that an age-old mantra that begins with the word "truth" could have an ending that could cause such a silly ruckus.

Guido Credo No. 8
The Truth: Ear relevant. It depends on whose ears.

The fictional heroes of my youth only ever had one "version" of the truth. If the police happened to arrive on the scene—with Lois and Jimmy in tow—before Superman could fly away, Superman's story did not vary, not ever. What he told the police is what he told Lois is what he told Jimmy.

The flesh and blood heroes of my youth, however, most definitely had versions. In the same scenario, neighborhood legend Dino "Ballbag" Bellucci (so named due to the ever-present bulge in every pair of skintight stonewashed jeans he owned) would have had three versions, even if he had done absolutely nothing wrong.

To the police he would have played up the "bad" guy's malevolence, turning up his own potential victimization.

The Lois of this variation, whose name would likely have either been Angela or Gina, would get a heaping helping of braggadocio. Had he simply slowed up his nemesis with an extended foot or headlock, it would easily turn into him having subdued him by extensive fisticuffs and possibly even something akin to Kung Fu, as it was sweeping the nation at the time.

The Jimmy would get the story closest to the truth, with an addendum delivered in hushed tones involving his belief that the guy he overpowered enjoyed it and was most definitely homosexual.

Inasmuch as mob activity and macaroni are inextricably linked to the Italian American, so, too, then is the truth, and their ability to bend it.

Guido Credo No. 9
Infidelity: Deny, deny, deny.

This might somehow suggest that a male of any other descent would come clean on everything from pick pocketing to bed hopping the minute he was asked. The need to purge, as it were, would outweigh any potential repercussions. Obviously, this is ludicrous.

(Although a good friend of mine has an Uncle Rocco who would tell you this was how confession came about.)

The most popular Italian American male response to a friend confiding that he had cheated on his girlfriend or wife and she found out, however, is indeed probably, "Does she have a picture?"

"Huh?" the penitent cheat will inevitably hiccup.

"Of you banging this broad. Does your old lady have a picture of you doing it?" his confidant will elaborate.

"Of course not!"

"Then deny it."

Surely many men have adopted this philosophy over the years, ethnicity notwithstanding. That said, though, perhaps only the Italian American male revels in the charade, to the point of making their significant other finally realize that the friend or relative who had told her of the indiscretion in the first place is an insidious, envious "hater," and never to be talked to again. Even more mind-boggling than the level of immaturity required to revel in such a thing then is the usage of the word "insidious."

This is why the majority of Italian Americans would prefer their friends not date their sister, and vice versa. It is a cardinal rule. Would Sonny Corleone have been able to hand out such an immense beating to his scumbag brother-in-law in

The Godfather—complete with knuckle biting and trash can lid to the head—were his brother-in-law also his best friend? More so, would that friend have been able to retaliate with the kind of set-up Sonny stumbled into were Sonny his best friend in return?

Hmmm. This has wound up being an argument *for* best friends dating each other's sisters.

Guido Credo No. 10
Siblings: You protect them from everybody. And nobody protects 'em from you.

We may have just inadvertently stumbled upon the very thing this chapter has been focused on. There could never be an Italian American superhero because if he were to have siblings they'd be a target for his nemesis, and no Italian superhero would simply turn a villain over to the police after he had hurt his brother or sister.

To paraphrase DeNiro in Brian DePalma's *The Untouchables*:

"Lex Luthor? Dead!"

"The Joker? *Dead!*"

"The Green Goblin? DEAD!"

Nor could you simply make an Italian American superhero's alter ego an only child like Bruce Wayne or Pete Parker or an adopted one like Clark Kent, because Italians never have only one child.

CHAPTER FOUR

A, E, I, O, U, and Sometimes Why the Fuck Not?

> ### Guido Credo No. 11
> There are two kinds of education:
> The kind on classroom seats and the
> kind on city streets. Ya know, one of
> them Road Scholars.

Studies show that Italian Americans are more likely than other Americans to live close to their relatives and to socialize with them regularly. And, also that Italian Americans put more of a value than many other groups on holiday customs such as summertime street festivals honoring patron saints. This being the case, Catholic school is the prevailing choice for most over public schools, if money allows.

Twenty-five years ago, long before two children per home became the norm, it was not unusual for a child to be in one grade and have a sibling in the grade below and another in the next grade, and also for there to be multiple cousins all around. In the seventies the norm for the average family was four children, minimum. Minimum! Simply put, a playground emergency that necessitated an immediate blood transfusion would not have been a problem.

Personally speaking, as the youngest of—yes—four, I had a sibling in each successive grade and was in the same grade as a first cousin all through school. A handful of second and third cousins (one of whom I would often inquire about the boundaries in regards to making out, which would repeatedly incur the wrath of my father's wooden spoon) populated grades behind me.

The pressure to learn is far more immediate for the Italian American, largely due to the length and lack of logic when it comes to their names. With a Johnson to your left and a Smith to your right, Italian Americans lag out of the gate, struggling to spell last names with, in most cases, more than ten letters, and wherein the sound "k" is typically spelt "cch" and so on and so forth.

A lifetime full of people mispronouncing your last name begins in the first grade. Shyness prevailing, correcting a teacher, guidance counselor, any authority figure, doesn't usually begin for another few years and is all but abandoned by your late teens, only to reemerge much later in life, particularly if you're miserable. An Italian American woman single and in her forties, sporting a goatee, will dole out a verbal lashing to a cop giving her a speeding ticket if he mangles her surname upon her handing him her driver's license.

(Interestingly, an Italian American woman will also hyphenate that enormous last name to one just as massive upon getting married, whereas an Italian American male would legally change his name to his nickname if he could.)

By the time the young student has mastered spelling his or her last name they will find themselves knee-deep in history everywhere they turn. Depending upon teacher and teaching style, homework can easily draw the ire of an ornery father. A take-home quiz involving the 1920s and 1930s, and more specifically, the domination of Italy by fascist dictator Benito Mussolini, can cause the same sharp tensions at the dinner table today that it did at the time in Italian American communities. Studying World War II, in particular, and the U.S. government's fears that Japanese, German, and Italian immigrants might betray their adopted country for their former homelands, proceeding to classify even naturalized citizens as "enemy aliens," could result in a diatribe over salad. Wherein, the other ethnic groups just mentioned are easily regarded as capable of such a thing, but just *thinking* it with Italians is an insult most unforgivable. That Italian Americans ultimately chose loyalty to the United States after it entered World War II in 1941 and declared war on Italy is the perennial double-edged sword for the Italian father helping his child with his or her studies. While the large numbers of young Italian American men who fought in World War II perceived themselves as totally American in the postwar years, such a skin shedding could be as difficult to swallow, even all these years later, as a botched al dente.

Nowadays, of course, school is a different animal altogether. Computers alone have most children ready to tackle those last names much sooner than their relatives were 20 years earlier. Again, however, the ornery, "off the boat" relative might come into play, potentially viewing the computer as a diabolical robot capable of eating his or her beloved 18-year-old cat, Needles.

> # Guido Credo No. 12
> Technology: Talk to me when they come up with the computer that can make a puttanesca and scratch my back after I'm done soppin' it up with the heel of a loaf of Italian bread.

There was a story in the news during the Y2K phenomenon of 1999 about an Italian woman living in a suburb of Massachusetts of either 86 or 87, who, in an effort to stave off impending financial ruin, extracted her grandson's desktop computer from its perch and launched it out his bedroom window. It only brought more, as shards of glass pelted a jogger who promptly sued the family. When the police arrived on the scene the old woman kept pointing at the demolished computer, shouting "Cattivo! Cattivo!"

Cattivo is Italian for evil.

And now, a brief listing of advances in technology that were begrudgingly accepted by most Italians over the years:

1) The crock pot
2) The kerosene heater
3) The electric blanket
4) The blender
5) The silencer
6) The "Clapper"
7) Electric car starter (A New Jersey "businessman" was

said to have motioned for the inventor of this gadget to get a street named after him.)

Even worse than the computer for the older generation of Italian Americans, however, is the cell phone. Not only is it a constant reminder of how poor their eyesight has gotten, but most regard talking on the telephone while driving an automobile as preposterous, and also yet another gigantic step in the continuing decline of Western civilization. Even when the best-of-intentions offspring is able to communicate that it is for emergencies only, meant to be stowed away in a glove compartment or the bottom of a purse, eventually a call will be missed and it will serve as a reminder of how poor their *hearing* has gotten too. A safety precaution, in short, will be regarded as an affront.

For every five or six Roosevelt-era Italians completely opposed to said invention(s), though, there is probably one or two who not only embrace technology but strive to abuse it as well. After all, a son or daughter giving such a gift and picking up the monthly tab is surely something to boast about at the Bingo parlor or, moreover, en route to the Bingo parlor. (There is a wheelchair-bound older gentleman in my neighborhood that has been spotted recently cruising down Main Street yammering away on his new cell, a swagger in the way he jettisons those wheels with his absurdly muscular forearms.)

Much like the cell phone, e-mail is something else we of the younger generation try to force upon the older.

> # Guido Credo No. 13
> E-mailing: There are better ways to send messages to people without them knowing who you are.

Admit it: The senior Italian American in your life is plopped down on a recliner covered in plastic watching *The Price is Right* at this very second, thinking Bob Barker has gone into the Witness Protection Program, and just waiting for the rotary phone next to them to ring. There's no shame in it!

Coercing him or her to learn how to log on and check/send e-mail is akin to asking them to get a matching tattoo of a Latin phrase in cursive.

Theirs is a generation sold on the face-to-face, the inventing of the telephone—and I'm referring to the rotary here!—still a relatively sore subject.

They also—perhaps rightly so—view such technological advancements as shortcuts when it comes to education. My father once saw a calculator in my backpack. He looked at me as if I was risking the entire family's collective life by harboring the compact fugitive. When I told him the teacher let us take our exams with it he was positively aghast. Had there not been a *Wiseguy* marathon on that night (the classic Ken Wahl television series) he'd have surely written a letter of complaint to the Board of Education.

With schooling also comes peer pressure, dances, dating, and so on and so forth. Rites of passage, to be sure, but also, depending upon the varying viewpoint of parents and grandparents, temptation not unlike the very apple that brought down the Garden of Eden.

Guido Credo No. 9
Drugs: Just say forget about it.

Italians by nature are not prudish. But they do view the ages of 14 and 15 as not all that different than eight and nine. Orthodontia is the sole exception. They will ask you why you are no longer bringing your teddy bear to school, why you're not wearing your Spiderman mask on the bus anymore. They wouldn't think of buying you a stick of deodorant.

By the time they accept the fact that you're not a bambino any longer it's because you got your driver's license and have become their unofficial chauffeur. Unbeknownst to them, you've already dabbled in marijuana and been treated for crabs. What's worse, gender bias thrives at dinnertime, among the clanking of the pots and pans, the breading of the cutlets; a daughter or granddaughter is expected to excel at her studies and hold hands until marriage, while a son or grandson gets a new baseball glove for a B minus and will be immediately nicknamed Romeo if he brings home two different girls in the same week.

This is where time-honored "street smarts" come into play, a branch on the educational tree one can either swing or be hanged from. Mastering vowels for a vowel infused last name is one thing, but navigating through the treacherous waters of puberty with the actual people who put the "old" in "old country" waiting for you at home is quite the other. And while Italians have no aversion to *eating* heart (artichoke; actual cow, which is called suffrito), there is an innate aversion to *having* a heart-to-heart. They talk, you listen. Period.

Of parents and grandparents, the latter is probably more likely to engage a teen in a talk about what they're struggling with at school, but their antiquated philosophies rarely apply. For every "lightning bolt" story there is one along the lines of "if you truly like a girl give her a goat."

(The "lightning bolt" reference pertains to a great scene in *The Godfather* when Michael is cooling out in his native Italy and spies a local woman and is immediately smitten. So perplexed is he by the intensity of his feelings for this veritable stranger, he is put at ease by an Italian comrade who tells him that he is merely experiencing the "lightning bolt" and that he should consider himself blessed, as it does not happen to just anyone.)

A grandparent will share the story above; a parent—fearing the potential of becoming a grandparent his or herself—will disconnect the cable TV in your bedroom and cancel any magazine subscriptions you may have.

Guido Credo No. 15

Grandkids are for old people or young people who raised either a dummy or a slut.

Like most homes, one or two grandparents either on premises or nearby is nothing but beneficial to the children, depending upon the grandparent, of course. Not only is there a real sense of family and heritage, but the wisdom and life lessons that could be at your disposal are nothing short of remarkable. After all, education begins in the home.

Many is the time advice from a sibling can be bested by advice on the same subject from a grandparent. (The actual parent is out of the equation at least until they are paying one's college tuition.)

Case in point: *A Bronx Tale*. (Yes, again!) When DeNiro's son seeks advice regarding a girl that he likes, he gets two decidedly different answers, although both, interestingly, come in the form of a test for the girl in question.

The first comes from a peer, his friend Mario, who creatively refers to the test as "The Mario Test." It involves taking the young lady for a ride in a car and getting on the highway. Then you are to pull alongside an eighteen-wheeler and get the truck driver's attention. Once you do you are to attempt to get the girl to fellate you. If she does she's no good and you are to break up with her immediately.

The other test comes from the Chazz Palminteri character, which is older, although not quite your standard "grandparent" age. His test is called "The Door Test" and involves picking up the girl in question, locking the car doors after you get out, and upon returning to the car with the girl in tow, opening the car door for her. Then you are to go around the back of the car and look to see if she leans over to unlock the driver's side door for you. If she doesn't, she is "a selfish broad and all you've seen is the tip of the iceberg." Again you are to dump her.

Guido Credo No. 16

Dating is like buying a suit. First you gotta try it on, and then you just alter the hell out of it.

Sidebar:
LEARNING HOW TO TALK TO GIRLS
(Italian American Style)

This particular lesson, as most Italians will tell you, can also come via an older sibling, but also from the hub of the young Italian American's universe: Church.

I absolutely learned how to talk to girls at mass on Sundays. Even though my family viewed church as, simply put, where you go Christmas morning after you've opened your presents and before you eat and eat and eat until you can't eat anymore (wherein you take a nap, only to wake up and eat again), I spent all of junior high going to church every Sunday for the 11:30 mass.

After all, every good-looking girl in the neighborhood was there. Not only that, they wouldn't be in their school uniforms, but in clothes they'd chosen to wear *themselves*. Isn't that reason enough?

I would take such advantage of the "peace be with you" portion, reaching two aisles up if need be, if that's where a pretty girl whose hand I wanted to shake happened to be. I was capable of hurtling a pew.

At church assemblies during the school day, we'd convene to sing our church's own songs or, at least, songs we presumed to be our own. Sister Louise and Sister Linda would be up there leading us, one of them accompanying on acoustic guitar. They were our very own habit-wearing answer to Simon & Garfunkel, singing songs with titles like "Happiness," "Take Our Bread," and "Lamb of God." Step one of my master plan was to sing these theatrically, my histrionics making everyone within earshot laugh uncontrollably.

When I began junior high the girls who brought the gifts every week were usually knockouts. I don't know how or why this was always the case, but you could bank on it; perhaps the selector thought this might translate to more in the collection baskets. Whatever the case may be, when the time came all the boys would be entranced, these girls in their tight jeans strolling towards the altar, one holding the wine and the other the communion wafers, nudging each other, struggling to keep straight faces. What's more, oftentimes it was girls who didn't even go to the Catholic school in the neighborhood but were instead two girls from catechism, students from the public school across the street who looted our well-kept desks once a week for school supplies and hidden candy.

After mass, everyone would congregate in the back of the church, mothers and fathers lighting candles for the dearly departed, and the playground just down the steps would permeate this holy place, the boys acting up in front of the girls. Sometimes, especially during Lent, they'd serve donuts and coffee (and hot chocolate for the kids) down in the church basement afterwards.

By the eighth grade I was an altar boy. I presided over

mass with one other altar boy, under Father Georgia. To this day, I recall the sensation. Being up there felt like what being on a stage must feel like, I remember thinking, Father Georgia with a chalice in his hands, held up high, versus (insert rock star here) with his Fender guitar raised in just as ritualistic a fashion.

After school one day during Lent, I had to clean up the church in preparation for a four to five o'clock confession period, and a mass at 5:30. Another student, two years younger than I and freshly permed from the hair salon, entered the church to ask what time the mass was. Her mother was out waiting in the car. We knew each other fairly well; she had complimented the way I doodled popular band names on my notebook, the way I made some look 3-D.

She had the curliest hair of any girl in the entire school, always left the top three buttons to her uniform unfastened, and aside from the fact that one of her eyes would occasionally move in toward her nose, she was really cute. I chatted her up instantaneously about the only subject I was remotely well-versed in and that she had already shown an interest in: Rock'n Roll. Or more to the point, I asked her if she would be attending a concert that was coming to town.

She said no, that she didn't have tickets, and her Hubba Bubba was intoxicating long before I'd truly get a grasp on that word. The next thing I knew I was asking her if she wanted to go. We were in church! I was convinced this was a violation of at least one of the Commandments.

Bless me father, for I have sinned.

I was keenly aware that asking her in church, of all places, the most sacred of places, and me being an altar boy, let alone a Catholic, was extremely inappropriate, but would the church hall be so different?

Though I am not worthy to receive you, only say the word and I shall be healed.

My hands began to tremble, beads of sweat ran down the part in the middle of my hair. And she said yes. Yes!

Give us this day our daily bread.

In retrospect I view this not as some potential sin, or act deserving of a lecture from Father Georgia at the time, but as a backhanded compliment to my upbringing and the Catholic church in general, 20 years before it would become the headline generator it has unfortunately become: I was comfortable there, truly comfortable. I honestly would not have been able to ask her on the playground or at the pizza parlor down the street. This was my home away from home growing up, just as I want it to be for my children now.

I asked my first girl out in church and she accepted. Too bad I didn't have tickets to that concert, or the money to buy them.

God from God, light from light, true God from true God.

CHAPTER FIVE
Wiseguys & Dolls

> ### Guido Credo No. 16
> It's not "money is the root of all evil," it's women with roots are evil. The blacker the roots, the blacker the freakin' heart.

What the word "roots" means to the African American community is decidedly different than what it means to the Italian American community.

To the former it immediately conjures up author Alex Haley's epic novel and, moreover, the record-shattering TV movie made of it in the 1970s wherein a young Levar Burton plays Kunta Kinte, and slavery was thrust into living rooms across America. It sparked long overdue and quite necessary conversation in the country.

To the latter it immediately conjures up the hairdresser as family member. It sparks long overdue and quite necessary stints under a dryer.

Italian American women take these roots more seriously than their actual roots (i.e. family history)! Furthermore, it is important at this juncture to note that Italian American women who prefer their roots as black as can be typically sport fingernails (be they fake or glued on) the size of a jaguar's. Are they not warriors seeking (and fully prepared for) battle?

In most cases, it is only an Italian boy's first love that is free of a mountain of curly, bleached, stiff hair with a strip of black down the center. Truly, "you never forget your first" means something entirely different to the Italian American male than to the female.

There are dueling Italian American beliefs when it comes to which is the more important rite of passage of a man's youth, the most telling: His first fight or his first love. The former has fallen in favor over the years, as many would like to believe that you should be able to go your entire life without resorting to brawling, but the latter remains an integral experience.

In the early half of the last century the kind of man you were going to be could be gauged by both of these scenarios, or so it was largely believed. How you approached an adversary, the level of courage, the willingness to stand your ground, and, ultimately, how you handled yourself if push *did* come to shove, was said to be a tell-tale sign of your true character. Ditto love in that a gentleman at 15 would no doubt be one his entire life, the potential for a broken heart changing that forever apparently highly unlikely.

> ## Guido Credo No. 17
> Fighting: If you are no good with your SATs, you better be with your FISTs.

Street-fighting as character assessment is an antiquated philosophy, to be sure. Although standing up for one's self is inarguably not only an important ability and something that is more than likely tested and determined during one's youth, that first fight, and its outcome, can eventually be overcome. A first love many times cannot.

Nonetheless, escaping your teens without gloves and loves is nearly impossible. Furthermore, on the Italian American home front, all of this activity is being duly noted. Inactivity even more!

By 20 if the young Italian American male has not been in love the immediate family will begin to suspect he is gay. (Having not been in a fight either doesn't help.) The young Italian American female is assessed as in need of an intervention, and a prearranged scenario will be cooked up as haphazardly as a ham pie on Good Friday.

No ethnic group has ever been keener on arranged marriages than Italians, and it is still happening today. The lonely bachelor living in America, with a family steeped in tradition behind him, can fly off to the old country and come back with a bride he has known for about as long as the stubble on his face.

Moreover, no ethnic group has ever been keener on marrying young than Italians. A guy who has dated the same girl since freshman year of high school could sell both sets of parents on a graduation/wedding combo if he were so inclined. Money and career are non-issues, as the hope looms that everyone will live under the same roof at some point anyway.

Guido Credo No. 18
"Nobody buys the cow if they get the milk for free" is bullshit. That's *how* the cow gets bought.

Dating is tricky terrain to begin with. Add to that a family equal parts overzealous and overprotective, and with a predilection toward saying things about "sleeping with the fishes" when it comes to your relationship not working out, and you have a recipe for (potential) disaster.

Furthermore, dating Italian is a decidedly different experience depending upon gender. A boy dating an Italian girl with brothers will invariably be threatened more than a poodle in a cage between two Rottweilers at a kennel. He will date in an almost constant state of fear. Ditto a girl dating an Italian boy, but in this instance the fear will be in relation not to brothers but to something far worse: the mother. (Editor's note: A recent study showed that an Italian mother can reduce a Rottweiler to a quivering mass of yips merely by staring intensely at it.)

A boy dating an Italian girl, his ethnicity notwithstanding, can ingratiate himself much more easily than a girl dating an Italian boy. Bring the newspaper up from the curb, snug under your arm as you ring the doorbell (honking the horn from your car as you pull up is a ticket back to bachelorhood); pop the top back on the garbage can and drag it up the driveway; eat when it's offered, and do so heartily.

Contradictorily, a girl who takes it upon herself to wash the dishes after a meal may as well spit in her boyfriend's mother's face. Fasten your seatbelt, sister, and simply hope for the best. (Case in point: An unintentionally hilarious episode of the short-lived "reality" series *Growing Up Gotti* wherein Victoria endeavors to set her sons up with "nice Italian girls" she'd like as potential daughters-in-law (surely the term "cherry-picked" has never been so loaded with double entendre).

In any event, once taken somewhat safely under the wing of an Italian American clan there is one major test down the road: the holidays. The holidays are to dating an Italian what the bar exam is to those studying law. Unlike the bar, however, you cannot study for this, cannot truly prepare yourself.

Let us begin with Christmas Eve.

The menu will consist of fish. Fish, fish, and more fish. Fish to start with, fish as the main course, and—as soon as some baker can master it—fish cannolli for dessert. Perfect a squid-flavored coffee and you'll drink a calamari espresso afterwards. In short, allergies be damned—sock some Benadryl away and prepare for the swelling. Asking for something other than what is being served, even with a horrific tale of having eaten shrimp and being in a coma for several days afterwards in tow, is the same as asking to be shown the door.

Guido Credo No. 19
Burping is a compliment to the chef.
A fart is sending a thank-you card.

A gentleman caller can bring flowers for the girl's mother on Christmas Eve. A young lady dating the son of the house can bring something she prepared herself in the kitchen. Not being able to cook is worse than illiteracy. Again, however, this is tricky; do not—I repeat, DO NOT—outdo his mother. While you do want to show your finesse with a whisk or spatula, and bask in the resulting kudos, you do not want to outshine mom. Best advice: Go heavy on the salt. Like an entire shaker heavy.

Christmas Day is considerably easier, with the gift giving aspect being your main concern. In fact, your only other real concern is wardrobe. A man who slathers on bad cologne will be asked if he thinks he's dating a "French whore"; a woman wearing a short skirt will be asked if that's what their son is dating.

Whenever I exchanged gifts with girls I dated as a youngster it typically occurred after a brief visit with the family, alone out on the front steps under a starry New England Christmas night, or in the family room as "The Year Without a Santa Claus" hummed on the television. But not the Italian girls! Here the exchanging happened in front of the entire family, down to relatives you're meeting for the first time, half-dead great aunts rolled out in wheelchairs who punctuate everything that gets said with a loud, disgruntled "huh?" or "what?" Their agitation grows exponentially throughout the proceedings.

There is a degree of performance expected. You have to be completely moved by the thoughtfulness behind each and every gift, down to the specific words underlined in the card accompanying your lot.

And the "first-timer" in this situation is going to be plenty surprised when the show begins and he or she realizes one or more of the gifts they have brought over is of a..."personal"... nature. Gag gift takes on a whole new meaning.

A list of what a man should **not** give a girl (in front of her folks anyway):

1.) Victoria's Secret gift certificate

2.) CD of gangsta rap.

3.) Pearls (her Nana will have a faux heart attack, exclaiming that "pearls bring tears!!").

A list of what a girl should **not** give her guy:

1.) Rogaine

2.) Chest and/or back-waxing gift certificate

3.) Crabs

While Christmas is the equivalent of one's bar exam, Easter is certainly right up there. Doling out palm on Palm Sunday is a class move for the suitor, especially if he gives some the size of a loaf of bread to the surviving grandparent who still acts as if their spouse just died a few days earlier, even while it's been approximately 20 years. (Sidebar: This grandparent will also be visited quite often by their dead spouse, who will be visiting, ostensibly, only to give the next day's lottery numbers; do not be alarmed.)

Guido Credo No. 20

Lent makes up three quarters of what Saint Peter has on ya at the Pearly Gates. If you blew giving up tequila when you were 27, it's on there.

It is also important not only to give up something for Lent, but also that it be something that is very much a part of your daily life. Giving up, say, coffee when you're not even a coffee drinker makes you no different than those who stoned Jesus in the eyes of your new love's parents, two sets of eyes with eyebrows already arched at your heritage-impaired generation. The wiseguy gentleman caller who gives up reading when he doesn't even do that with directions could get hit in the head with a Bible.

To further complicate matters, giving up something that is truly a part of your life (and difficult to abstain from to boot) but ultimately reveals what can be perceived as a flaw— is trouble as well. To wit, a boy who is asked by his new girlfriend's parents what he has given up for Lent and answers "the tanning salon" may be doomed. Equally the girl who answers "clubbing every night."

Thus, some "safe/smart" things to give up for 40 days and 40 nights include but are not limited to: Candy, gum, soda pop, beer, and cursing.

It is also imperative that you do your best to stay on top of the "no meat on Fridays during Lent" rule. Volunteering to bring the pizza one Friday when your girlfriend tells you her family is planning on having that for dinner is a stroke of genius; flipping it open to reveal greasy pepperoni that a non-English speaking grandparent will say is made from Lazarus's pig is the same as saying you want to see other people. Even worse would be to obliviously witness every family member order seafood while out at a nice restaurant and proceed to order steak. "Scrod, calamari, swordfish, porterhouse" can actually turn out to be your very own Last Supper. Literally.

Sidebar:
PIZZA TOPPINGS: WHAT THE FUCK IS GOING ON?

I am quite certain I speak for every Italian out there when I say, "Calm down with the crazy pizza toppings, people!"

For the sake of full disclosure I will tell you that I do occasionally enjoy a ham and pineapple pie (effectively known as the "Hawaiian"), and it was an instance when I ordered a slice that I first began to realize that pizza toppings were and are totally out of control. I was out for lunch with a friend and his crotchety father who, upon overhearing my order, declared such a pizza "an aberration." While indeed tasty, his palpable disdain led to rumination.

Easily the most scandalous of the lot has got to be chicken. It simply has no place on top of a pizza, and BBQ sauce in lieu of tomato should render the orderer ineligible to ever enter Naples in his or her lifetime.

Some other offenders: Jalapeno, feta, anything green (spinach, broccoli, etc.), hamburger, steak, mashed potato, avocado, some bizarre breakfast variation wherein scrambled eggs and bacon are present, and lactose intolerant cheese (a conundrum, to be sure).

I do not wish to be an alarmist, but if we do not nip this pizza topping trend in the bud right now, I fear these future toppings: Cauliflower, raisins, pistachios, cherries, potato chip debris, belly button lint, and thawing meat juice.

A common thread for the Italian American throughout all of this—dating, romance, adolescence in general—is dancing. Throughout their entire lives, actually. Michael Flatley may be "The Lord of the Dance," but John Travolta's hoodlum trifecta of Vinny Barberino, *Saturday Night Fever* and *Pulp Fiction* put the Italian-as-dancer on the map ("Crimelord of the Dance?").

Interestingly, what few people know is Travolta's *Saturday Night Fever* was not born in a movie studio pitch session, as coffee-swilling executives watched a *Welcome Back, Kotter* marathon (After all, had that been the case, Ron Paolillo—aka Arnold Horseshack—might've wound up playing Luke Skywalker). Rather, the film was hatched from a *New York* magazine article about what the journalist described as "disco crazy Italian American kids from Bay Ridge, Brooklyn." The title of the article was "Tribal Rites of the New Saturday Night." by an English rock critic no less, and followed a group of working-class Italian Americans who were as good at fighting as they were at dancing.

> ## Guido Credo No. 21
> Music does soothe the wild beast.
> Plus, it's great to bang a broad to.

The Italian American male knows the importance of dancing when it comes to wooing a woman, but also revels in the spotlight, oftentimes dragging a bashful gal onto the dance floor kicking and screaming, similar to an amorous caveman. Somehow, while saying "I love you" is the hardest thing in the world for many Italian men, pointing straight up at a strobe light on a dance floor and proceeding to shake your ass is not.

Thus, kicking off your marriage with a night of dancing at your wedding is regarded by many as more important than even consummating it. Ritualistic, to say the *very* least. The groom will totally be more interested in displaying stamina on the dance floor than anywhere else.

> ## Guido Credo No. 22
> A wedding is a chance to throw cake
> and not be told you have no class.

Truly, an Italian American wedding isn't all that different from going to a nightclub: lots of dancing and a couple of fights.

An article in a New Haven newspaper ran in the late 1980s about an actual stabbing cover-up at a wedding. Bad enough there was a stabbing, but an attempted cover-up? Only an Italian could come up with this as solution.

To victim: A boner while dancing with your cousin's wife? You deserve that cut, you mutt.

To attacker: Dump the knife in the sewah.

To on-looking busboy: You didn't see nuthin', capeesh? If you did, your eyes wind up on my keychain.

The owner of a local drycleaners was interviewed. He had inadvertently (or so it would appear) held up the investigation by not being able to differentiate bloodstains from tomato sauce. The victim's shirt had been tossed, but not his friend's, who, in holding his wounded goomba, added blood to marinara.

To really capture the essence of an Italian American wedding is to border on parody, however. Inasmuch as Greeks can say *My Big Fat Greek Wedding* nails every detail, the scent of spoof lay all over the film.

While easing tensions in relation to stereotypes is the ultimate goal of this book, it is tempting to run with them at times, and weddings are the biggest and best target for pretty much any and every ethnicity. Those over-the-top stage shows with titles like *Tony & Tonia's Whackjob Wedding* that permeated buffet halls across the country some ten years ago (and still linger) only succeeded in exacerbating the situation. An off-Broadway critic once referred to one as "toned down from its original conception." I can only imagine what the first draft was!

TONY & TINA'S WHACKJOB WEDDING, ACT ONE

LIGHTS UP

INT./EXT. TONIA'S FRONT PORCH
TONY DiFRANCOCARMEGLIO, a 22-year-old lanky boy with wavy black hair loaded with product, is pacing nervously. TONIA CRISCUOLODEBENEDETTO, same age, seemingly isn't even noticing, snapping bubble gum ferociously and inspecting her freshly done two-inch-long fingernails.Her clothes areskintight, her hair piled high on her head.

TONIA
Ton, huh? Yer makin' me freakin' dizzy ovah here.

TONY
I got shit on my mind, Ton, a'right? Don't break my balls!

TONIA
Break your balls? Maybe youz want I should leave you alone all togeddah, huh? How 'bout that?

TONY
I want just the opposite, baby.

Tony plucks a tiny jewelry box from his pocket.

TONIA
Are...you...serious?

TONY
You bet your ass I am.

TONIA
I mean that you're not gonna openthe box for me, you mamaluke.

Tony sighs and opens it.

TONIA *(continuing)*
Maaaa!! I'm gettin' married!

CUE music.

Opening Number: "I WAS GETTIN' OLD (BUT NOW I'M GET-
TIN' MARRIED)"

TONIA *(continuing)*
My father said don't give the milk fer free/Hey Dad
lookit me/Just last week we was through/Now I'm en-
gaged at 22!

TONY
Over that threshold thing yer gonna get carried...

TONIA
I was gettin' old, but now I'm gettin' married!

TONY
Me an' you, husband an' wife...it's gonna be the
bomb...

TONIA
In 20 years I'll look just like my mom!

ENTER Tonia's mother, an enormous, hirsute Italian
woman in a bathrobe and toting a rolling pin. Tony
faints.

LIGHTS DOWN

Quick set change.

LIGHTS UP

INT. - WEDDING HALL
The freeway can be (seen and) heard just outside
the window of an enormous hall, filled to capacity.
Voices are louder than the deejay himself, who is
frantically trying to get everyone to quiet down in
order to introduce the wedding party.

Among the things heard:
GUEST 1
The fried mozz is the balls!

GUEST 2
I don't give a fuck if it is a wedding, I want my
money!

GUEST 3
Yo, Geno! Massimo just told me he banged Tonia! I freakin' knew it!!

Finally, the deejay is able to get them to simmer down. He has begun to play "The Macarena" and it's like a veritable tranquilizer dart that disables the entire crowd just long enough for him to begin his announcement.

DEEJAY
Now that I have your attention. It is time to introduce the wedding party!

CUE entrance music.

DEEJAY *(continuing)*
First, the grandmother of the bride and the groom's cousin. Fortunato Belladonoccio and Giuseppe DiFrancocarmeglio.

Giuseppe, a gym rat who clearly spends as much time on his pecs as he does his goatee enters like he's the main attraction, initially forgetting that he has to wheel the bride's grandmother out. He rushes back and then returns with her. She is positively catatonic, but the roar of the drunken crowd stirs her. She stiffens, sitting upright.

GRANDMOTHER
Did my numbers hit? *(she looks upward)* My beloved Alphonse...you gave me the winning lottery numbers.

Quickly wheeled off to the side, the deejay continues.

DEEJAY
The parents of the groom, Anthony DiFrancocarmeglio, Senior, and Etta DiFrancocarmeglio.

Tony's mother attempts to enter gracefully, but Tony, Sr. is tugging at his balls, per usual, and gets a ferocious nudge from his wife of 25 years. Then he checks out a scantily-clad guest a bit too long and the nudge turns into a full-fledged elbow to the gut before Etta storms off.

TONY, SR.
What!? Lookin' ain't touchin'...we talked about dis!

GUIDO'S CREDOS

DEEJAY
Okay...um...the parents of the bride, Anthony
Criscuolodebenedetto and his wife, Antonia.

They enter much more restrained.

ANTHONY *(out of the corner of his mouth)*
Lookit all these goddamn moochers. I ain't payin'
for all o' dis, Toni.

DEEJAY
The Maid of Honor, Francesca Buonocorianno, and the
Best Man, Lincoln Carter III.

*Francesca and a smiling African-American Lincoln en-
ter and the applause stops abruptly.*

DEEJAY *(continuing)*
And now...for the first time anywhere...

*STAGE LEFT Tony can be seen picking his nose and
flicking it, while Tonia has compact out and is fe-
verishly tweezing between her eyebrows.*

DEEJAY *(continuing)*
Mr. and Mrs. Anthony DiFrancocarmeglio, Junior!

The crowd roars as Tony and Tonia ENTER.
CUE music: Bon Jovi's "Livin' on a Prayer."

DEEJAY *(continuing)*
The couple have chosen Jon Bongiovi's "Livin' on a
Prayer" to dance to for their first dance as husband
and wife.

*On one side of the stage a group of guests a playing
dice, and on the other two couples are doing blow.*

*Music and lights FADE. A hundred forks proceed to
clink against glasses in the dark. Then lights UP,
and everyone is now seated. Meathead Giuseppe rises.*

GIUSSEPE
I guess it's dat time. Da toast.

Everyone cheers. Lincoln gets halfway up.

LINCOLN *(smiling)*
And that's the best man's job, right?

A pin drop is heard.

LINCOLN
Why don't you go ahead, Giussepe?

GIUSSEPE
Ya tink so? Where do I begin?

He reaches over and grabs Tony by the head, messing his hair. Tony smiles.

GIUSSEPE *(continuing)*
Dis guy. I love dis guy!

He shakes Tony's head even harder.

TONY
Zep, huh? The hair!!

GIUSSEPE
I remember da foist time Tony laid...hey, get yer minds outta da guttah! Laid eyes on Tonia...

The crowd laughs uproariously.

GIUSSEPE *(continuing)*
I'll nevah forget his words. "I wanna break me off a piece o' dat."

The entire crowd, like a chorus: "Awwwwww." Giussepe wipes a tear from his eye.

GIUSSEPE *(continuing)*
How far off can a couple o' bambinos be, am I right?

The crowd claps ferociously.

TONIA
I'm late right freakin' now!

The claps turn into cheers.

GIUSSEPE
Kiss yer wife you fuckin' cavone!

Tony and Tonia kiss, tentatively at first, and then with more passion. It turns, of course, into a full-on makeout. The crowd begins chanting: "Speech! Speech! Speech!" Tony rises.

TONY
I don't know what to say here. I just hope to do
half as good a job lovin' Tonia as my old man did
to my Ma.

CROWD
Awwww.

ETTA
And all of my friends.

TONY, SR.
Etta, baby, don't be like that...

He reaches for her arm but she jerks it away.

TONY
Although, Tonia's spaghetti and meatballs will never
be able to touch my muddah's!

*The crowd laughs but Tonia is irritated by the com-
ment, which Tony sees.*

TONY *(continuing)*
In closing, I just have to say dat I'm the luckiest
guy on Turner Avenue in East Providence. And dis
little lady ain't gonna be able to walk right once
we get to Cancun!

*The crowd, again, cheers, no one more loudly than
Tony's father.*

TONY *(to Tonia)*
I love you more than life itself.

TONIA
I'll love you in death.

TONY
Yeah, well, I'll love you even when you're sick, and
you look nasty when you're sick.

TONIA
I'll love you even when you're sick, too, and everyone here knows how much you can stink up a bathroom.

TONY
I'll love you even after you blow out a few kids.

TONIA
I'll love you even after you get a gut from all your beer and braciole.

TONY
I'll love you even during the World freakin' Series.

TONIA
Yankees, Red Sox?

TONY
The balls on dis one!!!

CUE music.

Second Number: "MY OLD LADY'S GOT BALLS"

SPOTLIGHT on Tony.

TONY *(continuing)*
She don't take no crap/She won't shut her trap/She once pinned my ass on da floor...

GIUSSEPE
Pansy!

TONY
I'll tell ya dis/She's full o' vinegar an' piss/I won't be comin' home at quarter ta four.

Tony takes Tonia's hand and leads her out onto the dance floor.

TONY *(continuing)*
She once hopped outta her Firebird to call some guy a turd right at a traffic light/Barely five feet tall but my old lady's got balls and I don't mean she's a hermaphrodite.

CROWD
Awwww.

LIGHTS UP.

DEEJAY
And now, the father-daughter dance...for it the bride has selected Madonna's "Love Don't Live Here Anymore."

ANTONIA *(teary-eyed)*
From "Like a Virgin," our Tonia's first record. Her father bought it for her.

Tonia and her father Anthony meet on the dance floor. She is visibly chewing gum. They proceed to dance.

ANTHONY
You'll always be my little girl ya know.

TONIA
I know, Pop.

ANTHONY
An' I'll always be your daddy, no matter what. You only get one ya know. Take a look around here. There's all sorts o' people, but who's your daddy?

TONIA
That's hilarious. Tony's always askin' me "who's your daddy."

DEEJAY
And now the groom and his mother are asked to join the bride and her father on the dance floor.

Tony tosses a cigarette to the floor and stomps it out with his shoe. Then he meets his mom on the dance floor and they begin dancing.

ETTA
You look so handsome tonight, my Anthony.

TONY
Thanks, Ma. I meant what I said, too—about the spaghetti and meatballs.

ETTA
I know you did, honey. Promise me you'll do your best to be a good husband.

TONY
How can I not? I learned from the best.

Etta can see over Tony's shoulder that his father is making out with a waitress.

LIGHTS DOWN.

When they come back up a monumental wedding cake is CENTER stage. It is three-tier, and the frosting is gold colored. It appears to be littered with jewels. Tonia puts a piece up to Tony and he nibbles at it.

TONIA
C'mon, what's dat? You do tree pieces easy at Twin Oaks after the bars.

Now it is Tony's turn. He offers a piece to Tonia, who also nibbles gingerly.

TONY
Oh yeah, well, whadda ya call dat? I've seen you eat an entire Entenmann's before!

A few people laugh.

TONY *(continuing)*
I ain't kiddin'! Her crap had powdered sugar on it for days!

Tonia gets embarrassed. She grabs another piece of cake. She puts it up to Tony's face but he still only nibbles.

TONIA
Ton, huh? You can do better.

She turns to everyone else.

TONIA *(continuing)*
I guess there actually is one uddah thing Tony don't like to eat.

She smears it onto his face. The crowd cheers.

TONIA *(continuing)*
You won't bury your face in this, either?

Tony grabs a piece of cake and slams it into Tonia's face.

TONY
Eat up, Ton...why aren't you swallowing any? It's what you're freakin' famous for!

GUEST 3
No shit! Tell him, Massimo!

TONY *(to everyone)*
It was her yearbook quote, for Christ's sake!

Tonia punches Tony in the face. He punches her back.

CUE Music.

Third number (Entire Company): "LET THE CHEATING BEGIN"

GIUSSEPE
He says his bar days are over, but he's full of shit...

FRANCESCA
She was just as excited about Hairdressing School and in three days she quit...

GRANDMOTHER *(looking upward)*
This younger generation, all they do is fight...

TONY, SR.
I fucked a chambermaid on our wedding night.

CHORUS
Let the cheating begin, Let the cheating begin...

GIUSSEPE
This wedding party's full o' cows.

CHORUS
Let the cheating begin, Let the cheating begin...

ETTA
It does the minute he says his vows.

LIGHTS DOWN.

CHAPTER SIX
The Wizard of Schnoz

> ## Guido Credo No. 23
> Life is long and hard. Like spaghetti before you cook it.

Many married couples have confided in therapy/counseling that the biggest problem with their union is the fact that they feel they've been had; they were disillusioned, most citing "Hollywood endings" as the culprit. A scholar once noted—and I'm paraphrasing here—that people rarely think of life beyond the credits rolling. They do not think of what lay in wait for their favorite movie couple right after their joyous reconciliation at an airport, just before she was to fly off to Paris for good. Sequels notwithstanding, folks just don't know what to do when they get home from their honeymoon, ready to begin their life together, and reality hits them in the face, routine beckoning and romance slowly but surely beginning to trickle down the drain, masticated by the garbage disposal's metallic teeth.

The catch with the Italian American is while most people's versions of beautiful cinematic unions range from *Casablanca* to *Love Story*, theirs is, say, *GoodFellas*. Suffice it to say that the fawned-over woman is dumbfounded (though not entirely surprised) when the boyfriend or fiancé who romanced her, delighting in listening to her go on and on about her day, laughing outrageously at the most trivial of details and her accompanying idiosyncrasies, is suddenly the husband who delights in poker night and laughs outrageously at how loud he can pass gas.

There is a very tense but ultimately very funny scene in *GoodFellas*, in fact, where Ray Liotta's Henry Hill, married about a minute and living with the parents of his new bride (played by Lorraine Bracco), stays out all night, to the consternation of said parents. They ride Bracco mercilessly and eventually have her embarrassed enough to join them on the couch waiting for her husband to return, a chorus of "married men don't stay out all night" playing repeatedly. When Hill does finally show up, at sunrise no less, he is greeted by his wife and irate mother-in-law at the front door, the latter of who proceeds to read him the riot act. He simply breaks up laughing and gets back in the car.

Of course, it must be noted that Henry Hill isn't even a fictional character.

Though a couple's notion of their own Hollywood ending may differ, an even bigger hurdle comes in the form of children. That hook nose of his she found so adorable while dating is a source of major irritation when it is now looking back at her from the tiny face of their newborn daughter. Ditto the beauty mark on the Missus's eye that he once likened to Marilyn Monroe's that he now views as a "rat bite" on his little boy's mug.

Guido Credo No. 24
Moles: The only kind you have re-moved are ones with a heartbeat.

Noses and hairlines are the two significant causes for concern when it comes to bearing children for Italian Americans. As much as a boyfriend can eye his future mother-in-law suspiciously, praying under his breath that his hot girlfriend does not transform into the sideshow freak presently making him pasta fagiole, it is never lost on a girlfriend the fact that every uncle of her future husband is doing a comb-over a blind person would laugh at.

This is why Italian Americans are the number one providers and customers of toupees and hair weaves. Right now you are thinking of that one time you saw an obviously Italian man with what looked no different than a dead cat on his head, a "piece," a "rug" so obvious you immediately brought it to a friend's attention, asking him or her if this person honestly does not know how glaringly apparent this wig is.

He does not.

Again, he does NOT. Just as he is convinced the spear like hairs jutting out from his nostrils are invisible to the people he encounters on a given day, he is certain you think the animal corpse atop his head is his God-given, luxurious hair.

Even while plastic surgery has essentially become the norm, however, few Italian American men will get a nose job, or even think they need one. Were you to gingerly suggest to a fellow with a nose shaped like a pepper the strides made in plastic surgery, even delicately referring to his prodigious proboscis as nothing more than the result of a deviated septum, he would no doubt be shocked.

In short, when it comes to marriage, plastic surgery, wig critiquing, keep your advice to yourself.

Guido Credo No. 25

Advice is like when you're at the drive-thru: If you want a small fry, you'll ask for it.

It goes without saying that there is nothing more wonderful, no matter what the ethnicity, obviously, than the arrival of a little bundle of joy, of an Angelo, Jr. or an Angela.

(Sidenote: The Italian American couple can and will come up with a female version of any name if they have decided that their unborn child is to be named after a grandfather, father, etc., no mater how difficult the task. Giussepe will become Giussepiana before the first bouquet of flowers arrives in the maternity ward; Massimo will become Massimina; Ruocco will become Ruoccochelle.)

But, inasmuch as your bambino is a tiny mirror affording you the opportunity to perhaps truly see yourself for the first time, literal and figurative flaws and all, his or her arrival usually coincides with the first gray hairs, wrinkles (i.e. "worry lines"), and many other things associated with aging.

Keenly aware of this, as theirs has been a lifetime of their mother and father relaying (read: blaming) this very thing to them, this is why many Italian Americans prefer having children very young. Truly, though a good percentage of Italian American women might not say this aloud (and a bigger percentage will), their goal is to eventually be mistaken as their child's sibling.

At the local daycare or kindergarten the Italian American mother is easy to spot: She is the one dressed as if "Tiny Tot Daycare" is a nightclub.

Having children will also test your relationship. Yes, they create a bond that can never be broken between a man and a woman, but that does not mean hearts can't be.

Guido Credo No. 26
Love is a woman who'll put cream on your hemorrhoids.

Many parents adopt two mantras, the first being to never fight in front of the kids and the second being to never go to bed angry. There are literally millions of folks, stretched across generations, who will swear by this. None are Italian.

Let us begin with fighting in front of the children. In an Italian American home this will usually occur at the dinner table, otherwise known in an Italian home as the battlefield.

The triggers are many: lousy day at work, a mediocre meal, a screaming baby, a youngster refusing to eat.

I once heard that the number one household item used as a weapon in domestic disputes was the butcher's knife. In my home the most feared item was the wooden spoon. My father could wield it like a Ninja. His four kids would eye it nervously as it stood like a flag in the center of some baked ziti. One wrong word, groan…anything perceived as out of line and the old man could have it out of the ricotta and against the side of your head before you even had your napkin open.

This being the case, if the evening's fight doesn't begin as mother versus father, it can many times still get there thanks to an indignant child who has had enough Ronzoni to last him a lifetime, even while a narcoleptic grandparent will be quick to inform that he or she "once went three days eating only stale Italian bread and drinking dirty water in the old country."

So, going back to the wooden spoon/groan scenario, the father will proceed to hit the son in the side of the head with the underestimated weapon of mass destruction, only to be scolded by the boy's mother.

"Oh! He's only a baby!" she will say, nipping at some Carlo & Rossi.

"He's a baby because you baby him!" the father will respond.

"Only like your mother still baby's you!"

"Leave my mother outta this!"

"How can I? The cord is still freakin' attached!"

"Then maybe I should cut it! I'll use this!" (Father picks up knife.)

"You're scaring the kids, you cavone!" (She is unaware that the wooden spoon is far more terrifying.)

Ask any marriage counselor, therapist, or interfering in-law and they will undoubtedly inform you that this is a very popular argument between parents, the mother potentially babying a growing boy and/or the father not liking it, perhaps wanting him to "be a man" far too soon. It is all very common and normal.

However, said exchange would probably be encouraged to be had at bedtime, amongst the covers and paperbacks, softly and caringly, with the only possible weapon being a pillow.

The penchant for melodrama in an Italian American home is estimable, that scenario not nearly as exaggerated as you might think. Even more interesting is the very real probability that dinner would continue from that point on, not a leftover to be stored in the Frigidaire, work and school stories exchanged, with probably one or two more blowups before coffee/dessert.

Yet again you will be met with a look of complete and utter confusion if you were to suggest to an Italian parent not to argue with their spouse in front of the children. They would find it absolutely sinister to do it behind closed doors, to leave the kids out of it. To their way of thinking it is an Italian child's right to watch their parents fight.

Guido Credo No. 27

What we call normal conversation, you will most likely call an argument.

Moving on to the "never go to bed angry" adage.

Generally speaking, this is an impossibility for the Italian, as we are always angry about something. But, when it comes to this age-old rule of thumb, it is pertaining to a couple never going to bed angry...*at one another*. (This is still pretty near impossible, but for the sake of the text let's just use our imaginations.)

It is certainly a nice sentiment. The Italian American male practicing it, however, merely wants to have sex and will surely pick up right were he left off first thing in the morning anyway, and that's only if his wife has not spent the night hogging the covers or constantly nudging him awake due to his ferocious snoring.

Also, much like the dinnertime scenario, if children are not going to be a deterrent when it comes to an escalating disagreement, then a good night's sleep surely won't either.

"Shaddup already," the husband will say. "I wanna get some sleep."

"Why, did you only get 16 hours so far today?" the sarcastic Missus will reply.

"You wanna keep at it then, let's keep at it! I can go all night!"

"Maybe at arguing you can go all night, but not at something else!"

"Not with you I can't! I'd rather die!"

"I wish you would then!"

"Fine, beat me to death with this!"

"You brought the wooden spoon to the bedroom?"

> # Guido Credo No. 28
> ## 'Til death do us part can be arranged.

As documented earlier in the book, Italians really are strong believers in staying together, through thick and thin, even if both people in the relationship truly hate one another. What's more, the hate is actually anticipated, expected, even at times a source of great amusement. Or, at least, this was the case long before divorce became the norm, a feather in your cap to a certain extent, a badge of honor. First wives love nothing more than to say to the second, "Good luck to you!" Second wives get giddy saying things like "You must be a saint" to the first.

The main reason the older generation were such sticklers for adhering to the "'til death do us part" of the vows is for what I will heretofore refer to as "The Mourning Showcase."

"The Mourning Showcase" is when the widow or widower gets to wail over their dead spouse's corpse, beseech the Lord to tell them why, need to be pulled back and subdued, and then feast on antipasti until he or she falls asleep with half a black olive stuck to their cheek. This is a marriage's finale, the third act, so to speak.

While those in attendance at the wake will whisper to one another about a sobbing husband's infidelities or a weeping wife's famed white hot hate for the dead man, it is no matter. They have put in their time, put up with the deceased's peculiarities, endured thousands of nights sleeping beside someone they've grown to loath; now the spotlight is on them and you best be ready for his or her monologue. While the "key demographic" is their children, the showcase is really intended for all in attendance, everyone else gravy, and no one more so than the most recent widow or widower who really put on a show of their own at the time of their loss.

If at Frank "Cheech" Barone's services his wife threw herself on the open casket, then at the next funeral amongst largely the same congregation the possibility certainly exists that the widow-in-question here may flip the damn thing over.

My sister and I were once witness to a real lackluster "Mourning Showcase" and have referred to it often over the years. Due to that misguided attempt I will now lay out the steps to a definitive showing.

Five Easy Steps to the Best Mourning at a Wake

1) Attire MUST be all black, not so much as a gray sock. Red rose on collar/lapel is acceptable (and effective), but go the distance and wear black undergarments as well. During this performance, as you twist and contort your body "writhing in agony," chances are good your underwear may show at some point.

2) Pace yourself. Key word: Simmer. You need to bubble and pop like sauce on a stovetop throughout the entire wake.

3) In advance, pick a handful of people whose condolences will garner more of a reaction than others. Think carefully. Pick a former co-worker, a rumored "favorite" niece or nephew; it makes the showcase more believable, as those paying attention (which will be *everyone*) will see that you truly

knew the deceased, plus the handpicked "tear triggerers" will feel blessed.

4) The eulogy, aka the "For Your Consideration" moment: Let 'er rip. Moan like a wounded animal at certain points. However, never in the middle of a story. If the person doing the eulogy has decided to tell a popular story at the funeral the worst thing you can do is detract from it. If anything, howl at the outset rather than at the ending. It will suggest you were expecting the tale.

5) Open Casket. This is a must. Seeing their face is a necessity. If you truly ever loved him or her (in which case you've probably skipped this portion, as you surely won't need it) just seeing them will set you off, and if you've been waiting on this day much like you've been waiting to hear that Elvis faked his own death and is living in Palm Springs, their mug will drag your ire up from the depths, which you can use. If no one takes it upon themselves to wrap their arms around you and lead you away from the casket you will have to fall or, at the very least, stumble. Kohl's sells several nice black shoes, for both the male and female, that can facilitate a nice tumble.

Obviously I've gotten ahead of myself here. I went from having children to dying in a matter of a few sentences. (Many older readers are no doubt smiling to themselves right now, as they feel that's exactly how life goes.)

Death will be addressed again at the book's end, as my intention as far as the structure of the book is concerned is to begin at birth and go through the various stages of one's life. The previous portion was merely a discussion of one facet (read: bonus) of marriage, which this entire chapter is dedicated to.

So, in conclusion, and in returning to the married with children scenario, let us herald one of the major pluses: The tax breaks.

Guido Credo No. 29
Taxes: Death may be unavoidable, but...

In the popular area of New York City known as "Little Italy," on the corner of "Mulberry Street" there is a man who sells touristy items that I befriended one chilly November evening. I was there buying my newborn daughter a bib that reads "Not only am I perfect, I'm Italian too." The man said they were his second best-seller, and attributed it mostly to the locale. I asked him what his top seller was and he brandished one. It read "Papa's Little Tax Break."

It is quite possible that an infant can confuse April 15th with Christmas Day in the Italian American home.

CHAPTER SEVEN
Marconi & Macaroni

Once your Honeymoon Suite has officially been turned into a family room, toys cluttering the floor and in-laws clanking their coffee mugs together non-stop, it can be difficult to keep it together. The inbred love for tradition is what can oftentimes see the newlywed Italian American couple through this tricky period. Wanting your children to experience the same upbringing you did is a beacon of light in the darkness that is marriage. Passing on your heritage, legacy, and being focused on instilling a sense of values and a code of ethics (however "tweaked") is of the utmost importance to the Italian.

> ## Guido Credo No. 30
> ### Manners are for kids and first dates.

The only thing more important than well-behaved children is the *appearance* of well-behaved children. Squabble all you'd like en route to whichever relative's house you're on your way to—and all the way home for that matter—but when you're there you'd best be responsive to your mother and father. Being able to "read" your parents is an invaluable skill.

Many is the time the oblivious Italian child thinks he or she has gotten away with something simply because they weren't hit or even yelled at, but had they registered the glint in their mother or father's eye they would have ascertained that their beating was on layaway.

Truth be told, those early appearances as a family can be grueling. Every relative will invite you over for macaroni, to say no is the equivalent of spitting on *their* favorite dead relative's grave. The important thing is to embrace the fact that you are all in it together. Your mother and father are/were no more interested in Uncle Fausto's longwinded Italian history lesson than you. Those formative family years are nothing but Marconi and macaroni; best to regale one another with jokes about it and impressions of those relatives in the car. (Sidebar: Impressions are very important in the Italian American household; a report card loaded with D's is meaningless next to a spot-on Nana impression.)

Now that the (potential) downside to marriage has been effectively covered, let's discuss the (equally potential) upside. Yes, one does exist!

Just as easily as you can get a sister-in-law who does nothing but stir up trouble and bilk her sibling for cash, you can get one who is a peach. You can hit the lottery and come up with a babysitter/clothes-folding/kitchen wiz combo platter. Ask any Italian American and they will tell you your chances are probably 50/50.

You can get a drunken leech of a mother or father-in-law who is antagonized by everything that comes to you with ease or one who is your biggest fan, speaks broken English, and wants nothing more than to be a glorified servant in exchange for room and board in the garage.

Jokes aside, in most cases, joining two sizable Italian American families produces more positives than negatives. It can be a tricky course to navigate at times; choosing sides over tiny disagreements is never a good idea, for instance. But you will more often come up with a whole new group of people who will take a bullet for you and, even more importantly, for your children.

Merging two different ways of running a house is one of the more difficult aspects of being a newlywed. But, when two Italians marry said "ways" are probably already fairly close. An organized chaos, if you will. This is largely due to the fact that running a house is handed down from generation to generation to generation when it comes to being Italian. Hence, the continuing reign of plastic covering couches and recliners.

Truly, nothing is more of a powder keg than a dirty house.

Guido Credo No. 31

Cleanliness is not only next to godliness, it is the enemy of evidence, and that's a good thing.

Nothing brings a neighborhood block together more than a sweet domestic dispute. Sirens chirping (that stuttering way they do for domestics, as opposed to blaring), lights flickering, and every drape on the street being pulled aside. Ultimately folks pile out of their houses to whisper out of the corner of their respective mouths to one another what they think the ruckus is stemming from, and other things they've noticed lately and have begun to suspect. (Sidebar: When the family is Italian American, and one of the residents speaks in Italian at one point to the arresting officer it will absolutely confirm the entire street's suspicion that they are in the Witness Protection Program.)

The fact of the matter is, nine times out of ten a domestic involving an Italian American family will be either the direct or indirect result of a housekeeping issue.

Top 5 Things Heard on Episode of *COPS: Brooklyn*

5) "I haven't seen a pair of socks that f***in' match since we got married!"

4) "This pig thinks he can come home at four in the f***n' mornin' and track mud all ovah my carpet!?"

3) "Bitch acts like the Dust Buster'll give her f***in' cooties!"

2) "I couldn't get the s*** stains outta his undahwear with a f***in' Brillo pad!"

1) "If only da vacuum cleanah served vodka, right, you lazy slob!?"

This is typically the case largely because no room is more sacred in the Italian home than the family room. It is the epicenter of the home, more so than even the kitchen, if you can believe that.

Italian Americans will adorn their family room walls with countless photos of their children, as well as the wall that coincides with the stairs up to the second floor.

These framed photos will *never* come down. Ever.

If the parents cannot decide which photo to go with from a particular session they will simply purchase a frame that can accommodate every shot taken. They will update photos on an annual basis, including the family photo. Contrarily—or perhaps due to this—the Italian American family's Christmas photo will usually be a department store special at best (if not a Nana-and-her-Polaroid occasion, kids sitting and/or standing around the tree). A $9.99 department store special is irresistible to the Italian American mother, and she will be fully prepared to wait in line for 24 hours, waving her clipped coupon as if it's a backstage pass.

Using the upstairs bathroom in an Italian's home is to see the daughter of the house essentially grow up, from the newborn shot at the first step through the puberty and braces shot midway to the "I wanna be a freakin' model" phase at the top of the stairs (only to be bumped back a step if and/or when she gets married). Once the grandchildren are born they get a wing of their own, replacing framed photos of dead Italian singers ranging from Sinatra to Pavarotti.

Italians are likely to hang a "portrait" (not a photo yet not quite a painting) of a great, great, great grandmother adjacent to the television in the family room as well, and usually in the general vicinity of a statue of Mother Mary, as if to suggest they have several things in common. A bejeweled crucifix may be hung on a wall directly next to a framed family Disney photo. The juxtaposition of religious items with family photos is one thing, but in the Italian home a posed, professional shot holds the same value as the kids flipping the bird at the camera at Great Adventure, one of them wearing a "Damn Seagulls" T-shirt.

Other things you may spy hanging on the walls in an Italian American home, which can also assist in gauging the authenticity and severity of the Italian American*ness*:

1) A gigantic wooden fork
2) A "Rat Pack" collage
3) Framed advertisements for *Sopranos* cast meet-and-greets at area car dealerships
4) Glow-in-the-dark map of Italy
5) Massive Saint Joseph plaster

Another excellent way to gauge the authenticity and severity is by casually checking out the assortment of movies in the family room.

Guido Credo No. 32

Movies: If it ain't Scorsese it ain't shit. (But it's worth a shot if DeNiro or Pacino are in it.)

Some VHS still in the mix is usually a sign of the seriousness of the Italian, of the reverence, as with some vinyl and tape cassettes still stacked among the CD's.

Upon browsing the collection of movies, either on VHS or DVD, here are some titles to expect, in two entirely different yet very handy categories:

The Serious Italian American's Top Movies

1) *GoodFellas*
2) *The Godfather I & II*
3) *Casino*
4) *Donne Brasco*
5) *Once Upon A Time in America*
6) *A Bronx Tale*
7) *Saturday Night Fever*
8) *Rocky 1-3*

The "Cavone" Italian American's Top Movies
(All of the above, plus...)

1) *My Cousin Vinny*
2) *Mickey Blue Eyes*
3) *The Godfather III*
4) A random Danny Aiello movie
5) *Staying Alive* ("sequel" to *Saturday Night Fever*, "directed" by Stallone)
6) *Mobsters*
7) *Rocky 4-6* (and maybe even some *Rambo*)

Entering the Italian home can be disconcerting, unnerving—at first. Don't be ashamed of your nervousness. After all, they will think nothing of having a statue of a saint on the front lawn with running water coming out of a chalice in his hand. That's crazy!

I *am* Italian and was once mildly spooked by a girl-friend's home. Her name was Conchetta (which borders on overload right outta the gate) and her parents gave her a surprise baby brother right around her twentieth birthday. They may as well have named him Accidentio. I was used to the plastic-covered furniture and the homemade wine, both of which were present and accounted for (the fridge the wine got pulled out of may have even been covered in plastic, if memory serves), but it was the Italian children's book I spied that did the trick. *La Fata Del Dente*—near as I could tell—is a tale about a little girl who is jealous when her little brother loses a tooth and their mother tells him excitedly that the Tooth Fairy will be coming for it. This leads his envious sibling to extract a kernel of corn from an ear in the kitchen and paint it white, all in an effort to fool the Fairy. Apparently such trickery does not go over well with the Tooth Fairy, who promptly takes both kids to a land where the roads are made of teeth and legions of robots—yes, robots—work diligently to determine if a tooth is real or fake. I stopped flipping through the pages at this point, fearing a robot-as-decapitator scene a-coming.

Anyway, back to the text.

Once a family life rhythm is established it is tempting to attempt to pick up where you left off as far as a favorite pastime is concerned, to incorporate a lifelong hobby into the mix. Some prove easier than others.

Guido Credo No. 33
Hobbies are like a goomar (mistress): Everyone should have one.

For starters, golf for the male or, I dunno, knitting or bingo for the female. Bonding with friends is more important than ever, having an outlet where you can vent about situations at work and on the home front. What is key is to not try to "sell" something to your spouse as a hobby that clearly isn't.

Guys, going to strip joints is *not* a hobby, male bonding opportunity notwithstanding.

Ladies, neither is shopping.

One problem that can arise is that what was truly once a hobby has now become something you are expected to do. Women who have considered cooking a hobby can begin to actually loathe it once it has become their "chore." Ditto the handyman who used to relish the Saturday afternoon where he got to swing a hammer in all its phallic glory and build something and is now forever putting up a shelf or fixing a lopsided bureau.

While, again, these are standard occurrences in any marriage no matter what the ethnicity, Italian Americans already view spatulas and screwdrivers as weapons. While a man or woman of another heritage might take the time to run in the house to fetch their handgun or switchblade, and as a result have a moment to cool off or provide their spouse with the time to dial 9-1-1, the Italian American is already prepared to wield what's in their hand.

Top 5 Weapons Confiscated on Episode of COPS: Brooklyn

5) Empty liter of orange soda

4) Whisk

3) Remote control

2) Bottle opener

1) Hairspray canister/aerosol

It can be tempting to regret having gotten married, or myriad other decisions you've made in your life, especially in the time immediately following them. Fortunately for the Italian, regret is as much a waste of time as it is unacceptable. The Italian American male can confide to his "off the boat" father or—God forbid—grandfather that he has embezzled money from his place of employment and get a significantly lesser reaction than were he to confide that he regretted something.

This is essentially how such a scene would play out:

First Scenario

Son: Hey, Pa, can you mute *Law & Order* for a second?

Father: What is a the mute?

(Son reaches for remote control and after a brief struggle manages to mute the TV.)

Son: I gotta tell ya somethin'.

Father: What? Gagoots and eggs?

Son: No, Pa, I ain't hungry. It's just…I took some money from work. A lot of money.

Father: Ahhhh! *(Sobbing.)* Why can't a you behava you self? For a few dollars?

Son: Not a few, Pa. *Thousands.*

(Silence.)

Father: *(Conspiratorially)* Come, we put a behind a brick in the cellar.

Second Scenario

Son: Hey, Pa, can you mute *Law & Order* for a second?

Father: What is a the mute?

(Son reaches for remote control and after a brief struggle manages to mute the TV.)

Son: I gotta tell ya somethin'.

Father: What? Gagoots and eggs?

Son: No, Pa, I ain't hungry. It's just…I been thinkin' lately. I got lots of regrets.

(Father violently smacks his son on the side of his head, knocking him off the ottoman.)

Father: What's a matta' wit you?

Guido Credo No. 34

Regrets are like your goomar being at the same restaurant that you are at with your wife: best not to acknowledge.

Regret with regard to having a family is fleeting, to say the least, when you're Italian anyway. *La famiglia* is what it's all about, after all. The significance in Italian homes of good food and a big family cannot be exaggerated, and is even well documented. Take New Orleans, for example: it is the oldest Italian community in the New World, and saw the creation and rise of the *muffaletta*—which became what the city referred to as its "true Communion host"—even while the vigilante murder of innocent Sicilian immigrants was being ordered by the city's mayor and publicly condoned by the then-president of the United States. Still, la famiglia not only survived, it thrived.

The Legend of 'Meatball' Joey Pegs
(A Minor Digression)

Joey Pegs was an old guy who lived in my neighborhood when I was a boy. He was always walking around blurting out tidbits of Italian history. He couldn't have been much more than 5'2", sported an outrageous comb-over of greasy black strands that looked like licorice whips across his pink scalp, and was round enough to merit the nickname 'Meatball'. As a child I believed he was hit with the nickname stick twice, both the 'meatball' and the 'pegs', as the tiny little stumps that protruded from his oval midsection moved in the same symmetric fashion as a compass, knees apparently inoperable. In recent years, however, having met up with others from the old neighborhood for beers and reminiscing, one friend suggested otherwise; his belief is that the 'Pegs' was an abbreviation for whatever Joey's last name was, which is certainly possible and,

besides, nobody gets two nicknames that are actually said together. (Clarification: You can have several nicknames, used in
an alternating capacity, but not usually two *at the same time.*
Capeesh?)

Whatever the case may be, Meatball Joey Pegs was a legend, his arrest for urinating in public one Fourth of July just
one of many feathers in his estimable Italian cap.

He had an outrageously high-pitched voice—more like a
screech really, and seemingly never mastered the art of segue.
A bunch of us kids could walk past him and engage him briefly in a conversation about, say, the eggs-and-potatoes grinder
being served at the local sub shop that day and he'd go along
for a minute or so until he'd suddenly burst into a dissertation
about cobbling and its importance to Italy's fragile economic
infrastructure.

As we got older and began securing driver's licenses,
something alternately amusing and perplexing occurred. As
you drove by Meatball Joey Pegs, if you honked your horn
and shouted "Meatball" or "Joey" out the window he had a
sort of routine reaction. He'd wave frantically first, then pull
his pants up at such a rate as to suggest probable groin injury,
and then it seemed as if he spoke for a minute or so, even
though by this time you were at least a block away. It was later
reported by people within earshot that he would be simply
blurting out occasionally bizarre anecdotes relating to being
Italian.

Among the things overheard, if I recall correctly:

"Try driving like that on a cobblestone road."

"Where's the fire? Hopefully, in a brick oven!"

"Bad bowl of pasta fagiole going right through that one."

One Mischief Night—which is the night before Hallow-een and a standing night for pranks—a new kid in the neigh-borhood and a few of his friends pulled the ol' dog shit in a paper bag on the front porch trick on MJP. They lit it on fire, rang the doorbell and ran, only to watch from the bushes as Joe stomped it out and got the crap all over his shoe, to which he was no doubt oblivious. New kid furthered his stupidity by relaying the event afterwards, out in front of the corner store. The beating he got was also the stuff of legend.

By our early twenties MJP's mom had passed away and he got shipped off somewhere. Rumors began to circulate that Joe had served in three wars, WWII, Korea, and Vietnam. I immediately recalled a conversation I had had with him when I was around 14. It began with me griping about the New York Yankees.

"Joe DiMaggio's father wasn't allowed to fish in the Pacific Ocean during World War Two," he said abruptly, to which I had no immediate reply, outside of a pubescent giggle.

He then showed me a card the same size as a driver's li-cense, give or take, which referred to him as an "enemy alien."

CHAPTER EIGHT
A Skin Tag for Every Year

There is an old saying about telling how many years a man has lived by counting the gray hairs he has. This, of course, could never work on the Italian, and mostly because his hair is usually either a "piece" or colored. Thus, the "skin tag" is an alternative route.

A skin tag, for all of you laser removal whackjobs out there, is the redheaded stepchild of the mole, of absolutely no relation to the beauty mark. It is ornamental in the way that it hangs, a brown, movable "tag" that is typically the result of excess perspiration and as such shows up in spots prone to lots of sweat, i.e. the underarm area or neck. The older one gets the more he or she can be subjected to them, and the bigger they can become. My father had one under his left arm that was so big we kids named it. I genuinely miss Fredo.

The Italian male will address some byproducts of aging and simply ignore others. We've discussed hair implants/plugs/pieces, and now we will cover—albeit briefly—the only other "major" area the Italian will seek to rectify: Impotence.

To the Italian man Viagra is the greatest invention since the wheel. Some will probably argue it was even invented by an Italian, an inventor whose surname the very pill is named after, what with the vowel parked at word's end. In fact, I will now create an entire identity for you, dear reader, to help in perpetuating the mother of all urban myths!

Rocco Ottilio Viagra was born in Cleveland in 1955, the son of Osvaldo and Apollonia, a consigliere, racehorse enthusiast and homemaker, respectively. A chemist by his mid twenties, Rocco later stumbled upon the invention when attempting to treat his father's ailing horse, Sicilian Thunder, after the animal's veterinarian failed and was subsequently "relocated." Rocco did not succeed in helping Thunder to recuperate either, but for the last 14 days of its life it did have a massive erection. Osvaldo's very good friend Jack was CEO at a major pharmaceutical company at the time. The rest is, as they say, history.

Of course, there are other signs of aging that are as difficult to ignore for the parent as they are for the children. Pastimes/vices take their respective tolls: smoking cigarettes results in stained teeth and raspy voices; too much time spent in the sun results in brown spots and wrinkles; boozing results in hardened features and tremors.

Still, the true Italian will regard each of these "activities" with as much affection as they would their offspring.

> ## Guido Credo No. 35
> A man has two best friends: the bottle, and the person you call to drive you home once you empty it.

Furthermore, while older relatives of a different ethnic background will endeavor to give up smoking in favor of a daily walk at some point, eschewing the sun all together in favor of big hats and even bigger umbrellas, and at least feigning moderating their liquor intake, the Italian American will make no such concessions, our East Coast posse sporting an orange hue from tanning beds during the snowy season.

By the time your children are having children it can become easier to accept the fact that you are aging, to even embrace it to a certain extent. Once a grandparent, most Italian Americans even revel in it. Evidently a father who falls asleep at the dinner table is a drunken bum, but a grandfather who does is "endearing"; a mother who passes gas while watching *Wheel of Fortune* is disgusting, but a grandmother who does is "a real character."

Truly, the father who speaks in his native tongue when a child has friends over the house is a major source of embarrassment and told so, but the grandfather who does is either hilarious, adorable, or both.

Case in point, an actual scenario from my youth:

While over a friend's house one day, a girl called him on the telephone. His father, who was always working an Italian-English hybrid thing when it came to speaking (averaging three words in Italian to every two in English) answered the phone. We were right there in the living room where the phone rang, playing a board game on the floor.

Well, Dad handled "hello" and "hold on" just fine, but then he announced a *puttana* was on the phone for Michael without so much as cupping the receiver. Now, puttana basically means whore, and what's really disconcerting in telling the story is not that this father could use such a word in reference to a fifteen-year-old girl he had never met or heard a single word about, but that he said it in a way as if puttana simply translated to "girl." He was utterly casual about it.

Of course, Michael was more embarrassed that his father spoke Italian in front of me, and potentially in front of the girl on the phone. Whenever his father spoke Italian he felt it rendered him inferior in some way, and was always complaining that he should speak better English. Michael felt like people were laughing at him.

Nonetheless, Michael snapped: "Pop! Why do you even answer the phone?"

His father was clearly perplexed. He had his hands up in the air as if he were in a bank mid-robbery. Michael's grandfather came in when he heard Michael raise his voice (he lived there with them, in the basement where they had rigged up cable television illegally and where he was lulled to sleep every night via the chug of the washing machine and dryer).

Michael's father relayed to his father that Michael was on the phone with a girl is all, to which Michael's grandfather immediately grinned a deviant grin. "A puttana?" he queried quite loudly. Michael laughed hysterically.

In retrospect, maybe the laughing in this story was due to something else altogether, but you get the picture. Here then is a list of things that become acceptable and/or amusing once you cross the threshold from parent to grandparent, in addition to speaking another language in front of company:

1) All bodily functions. (Burping is downright riotous!)

2) As previously mentioned, narcolepsy.

3) Falling down.

4) Wearing slippers to a retail outlet.

5) Erections.

6) Stories about "the ol' days."

7) Forgetfulness.

8) Incompetence with regard to modern technology.

It will either be a major source of irritation or amusement when a mother or father sees *their* mother or father in grandparent mode, a smile greeting misbehavior rather than a smack in the head, a dollar being handed out conspiratorially when their wallet or purse had a combination lock on it throughout their child's upbringing. In short, when it comes to Italians, the transformation from parent to grandparent is easily as significant a transformation as that of a man becoming a werewolf by the light of a full moon.

More than likely the change in one's parent's demeanor will irritate, but it's not like they want to see their little one getting smacked by his or her grandparent; it's just, constantly hearing "why can't you be more like Grandpa?" and "Nana is the best!" and "Grandpa and Nana are so much fun!" is the equivalent of plunging a steak knife into the Italian American parents' respective hearts.

"Fun??" your mother or father will snap. "They wasn't fun when I would God forbid miss my curfew 'cuz a movie was longer than they thought 'cuz they couldn't read the freakin' newspaper and would pummel me around the Goddamn living room with a boot!"

This is potentially when you may see your mother or father cry for the first time.

The Italian grandparent does not want to reprimand, you see. Their sole purpose in their newborn grandchild's life is to provide them with shoddily-manufactured stuffed animals and see to it that they eat things like carciofo (artichoke). As the child gets older the stuffed animals turn into cold, hard cash (the average Italian grandparent will mail you a ten dollar bill for your birthday in perpetuity), and the carciofo into meatballs. They will sing in Italian unabashedly and will accompany the singing with outlandish dance moves just to make the child laugh.

When they were the parent and it was dinnertime, they declared "mangia" in a dictatorship tone, inferring that if you didn't yours was not going to be a splendid evening. As the grandparent they will deliver "mangia" in a singsong way, simultaneously twirling his or her mustache, much to the child's delight.

What's not to love?

Inasmuch as a grandparent is also viewed as a cash cow of sorts, a parent is equally expected to be a source of money, both when alive and posthumously.

Guido Credo No. 36

A will is an opportunity to tell someone to go fuck themselves from the grave.

For the Italian, there are two wills. First, there is the standard will, written up fairly quickly after having a first child and updated regularly. Second, there is the unwritten will, the one spoken in hushed tones, to either a wife or other confidant, a verbal treasure map that leads the "person in charge" either to where a family pet was buried, loose floorboard in the garage, etc.

The first will may be contested all you'd like, but the second cannot.

The will that is actually notarized may provide for some people no one in the immediately family has ever even heard of before, and the consigliere (lawyer) will have his own set of specific instructions on how to go about navigating this tricky course.

> # Guido Credo No. 37
> A consigliere is like a dog: every family should have one and, furthermore, one that bites and does not roll over.

A last will and testament for an Italian can be excruciatingly detailed, down to bizarre items ranging from "the menu from Cosimo's before that reptile fucked it all up" to a "set of dice that put the addition on the house" to the utmost in superstition, like a pair of lucky socks, "a must whenever I flew on a plane."

Interestingly, these random items can in many cases cause

more dissent than money and/or real estate. In fact, according to several attorney sources contacted for this book, the number one cause for arguments at a will reading for an Italian is jewelry. One attorney friend in particular—who requested anonymity—relayed a hell of a tale. (Sidenote: Requesting anonymity comes out of an Italian's mouth quicker than a dollop of tomato sauce when he realizes it's Ragu.)

He was reading the will of an extremely wealthy Italian restaurant owner in Connecticut, and to an enormous family to boot. The way he put it, he was "doling out real estate like we were all playing a game of Monopoly." While the recipients of property as diverse as a cottage on the shoreline to an apartment building wherein one of his cafes occupied the first floor were certainly moved by his generosity, embracing one another teary eyed, the attorney said he sensed they would all prefer the deceased were still with them rather than acquiring this new property.

But when he got to the jewelry of the will the tears dried up and fangs emerged. One ring specifically, described to me as a huge, "mood ring looking thing," caused an actual fistfight, and another, with the deceased's initials in an elegant cursive across it, was left to the son with different initials. When it was suggested "Pop was outta his fuckin' mind obviously. Why would he leave a ring with his initials to you, when my initials are the same?" the attorney had to step up and reiterate he was of sound mind until the very end, that they all knew it, and that he had explained that the son he was leaving it to had always admired it.

"Even so," was all the disgruntled same initial son could think to say.

"I'll change my fuckin' first name," his brother suggested facetiously. "How's that sound, you fuckin' mortadell'?"

Fistfight number two.

Yes, two fistfights at a will reading! And not over the discovery of a sibling one never knew they had, or the leaving of property to a goomar, but over jewelry. What's more, jewelry that my attorney described in this way: "Big as bugs from the Congo, some of which may have been battery operated, as one of the rubies looked like it could light up."

Of course, all of the proceedings and resulting behavior/reaction is directly affected by the way in which the person has passed on. If it happened to be the result of a violent act, all contempt and hostility is saved for those responsible, and certainly not for one another.

However, if it was due to a long illness, wherein there was enough time for siblings to keep track of who did more for the dying parent, well, quite frankly, you may as well read the will at a police station.

Guido Credo No. 38

Cancer is like an asshole mother- or father-in-law: It can come without any warning whatsoever and you have to get rid of it before it kills you.

The dying Italian male is positively Shakespearean. This is not to suggest that he will suddenly be speaking eloquently, the onset of the dying of the light providing enough of a flicker so as to suddenly be adept at turning a phrase; rather, the melodrama and potential for dementia-induced disclosure that may rock a family to its core is enough to keep Central Park booked up for many a summer to come.

He will be certain he is in the throes of his final breaths quite some time before he actually is, and is completely capable of putting his family through *several* trial runs—sometimes inadvertently and others completely aware. He is the one in Hospice exclaiming "this is it, this is it" while panting heavily and clutching the closest person's hand with the hand he isn't using to place over his own heart.

Oftentimes a family will begin to mourn, only to be shocked when the presumed dead will suddenly quip "You call that crying?" or "You're blocking the TV."

A bedside vigil is absolutely mandatory, anything else the equivalent of urinating on his grave, and he will say as much. Even taking shifts, as some families are forced to do when an illness lingers and work and school schedules can no longer be left in the lurch, is a slap in the face. The family representative will often be greeted with zingers marinated in sarcasm: "Lucky me, look who got the night shift" or "Well, well, here comes my favorite part-timer."

Ideally, Italians prefer to die at home, in their own bed. A hospital or Hospice is, to him, merely "Heaven's waiting room," and alternately flipping food trays over and flirting with nurses is par for the course.

Some loving (if a bit misguided) children who selflessly

turn their living room into a hospital room for their parent will resurrect the intercom they used for *their* children in these cases, enabling the old man to turn his son or daughter into a concierge. Digging the intercom out of storage is a nice gesture, to be sure, and definitely a smarter move than giving your parent a bell or some equivalent. Giving the patient the opportunity to be a percussionist is just plain stupid.

In an effort to yet again look at a potential upside of a situation, as opposed to dwelling on the downside (and using the word "upside" in this type of scenario is stretching it, I know), let us assume who you've got in the spare bedroom droning on about what a miser you are when it comes to the heat wants to go out imparting wisdom. This can be as likely as the melodramatic, odious version.

A deathbed pep talk can literally, if you'll excuse the pun, last a lifetime. It carries an extra weight, obviously. Either if the person passing on the rumination has practiced what they're preaching or if the exact opposite is true and they are realizing where they went wrong in a certain situation and want to make sure that you don't, truer words will probably never be spoken to you. Only—I repeat, ONLY—if the person dying is an unabashed bullshitter and giving advice they'd have stuffed back down the throat of someone who attempted to give it to them should you take it with a grain of salt.

The heart-to-heart with the person who has done everything they are telling you to do—no, imploring you to—can occasionally culminate in a variety of somewhat bizarre, oftentimes open-ended, homemade clichés. What is being said will sound like something you once saw on a bumper sticker, but after countless hours analyzing it you will realize nothing was really said at all.

These include but are not limited to:

"Go after everything you want with everything you got or in the end what are you?"

"Sometimes it feels like the whole world's against you, and sometimes it is!"

"Believing in yourself is very important because...well, you're here, ain't ya?"

"You get more bees with honey, but those fuckers sting!"

"Dreams are important, but daydream and people think you're stunad."

Still, even if those final words are more riddle than revelation, it is probably of the utmost importance to the person saying them that you react as if they just whispered the whereabouts of the Holy Grail. They are spending their final hours simultaneously stewing about things and pondering if they truly reached their potential, obtained their goals.

> # Guido Credo No. 39
> Goals: No different than hockey. If ya can't obtain one, pull the jersey over someone's head.

By simply writing this I can see now that—at least in my case—the person who wants you to learn from their mistakes, as opposed to the one who went after everything they wanted to in their life, might utter sentiments that are a bit more cohesive, if only due to the fact that learning the hard way might bear more fruit.

The heart-to-heart with the person like this, however, can occasionally culminate in a variety of somewhat bitter, oftentimes curse-fuelled, homemade clichés.

These include but are not limited to:

"You only live once; don't waste it on an asshole like I did."

"Life can blow, and your girlfriend should too."

"Home better be where the heart is if you're like me and you marry a heartless son-of-a-bitch."

"If at first you don't succeed, don't crawl into a bottle like someone else we know."

CHAPTER NINE
A "Wop"-ping Good Time

The goal of this book—like life itself—is merely to have a good time, as many laughs as possible, to not be so uptight and, mainly, to be proud of where you come from; proud enough to poke fun at it and even appreciate the fact that some things are so ingrained in a given ethnic group as to immediately conjure up said group upon merely hearing certain words.

Let's play a round of Ethnic Word Association, shall we? But instead of me giving the answers, you can just fill in the blanks at home. (That should keep the death threats at bay.)

Mobster.

Cheap.

Drunk.

Can you match up the word with the "appropriate" ethnic group? Of course, this is not to say there aren't cheap Irishmen out there or drunken Italians; I know several in each category (although I have yet to hear so much as a word about a Jewish mafia)! But, if you connected the dots, so to speak: Congratulations!

I congratulate you not on getting my silly quiz right, but more so on playing along in the first place, on not being such a tight ass as to let political correctness rob you of your sense of humor and, yes, heritage.

Why is it that when there is a hilarious scene in a movie

about Italians, row upon row of Italians will stop laughing the second they notice, say, a black or a Mexican laughing, too? Ditto a funny scene in a Spike Lee movie when a white guy in a Gold's Gym tank top reeking of Cool Water cologne joins in the laughing fray? We're saying "it's okay *for us* to laugh but not you." Laughter is the last thing that needs segregating.

But, to reiterate, anything said with hate, any derogatory term issued with venom, is another story entirely, and there are laws against it for a reason.

Interestingly, oftentimes it is an organization made up entirely of the very ethnic group that is the focal point of a series or film that raises the fuss. In all of the years *The Sopranos* reigned on HBO it was myriad Italian American groups that cried foul, citing characterizations as "insulting" or "inflammatory."

I have taken the liberty of writing...er, I mean *compiling* several letters of complaint that I managed to get my hands on, sent to an Italian restaurant in response to a commercial they had cut to promote their new menu. Evidently the tongue-in-cheek aspect of it was lost on the letter writers, who, in their haphazard attempts to beat back stereotype only managed to reinforce them.

* * *

To Who It May Concern,

I saw your new commercial the other day during a break on *The Tony Danza Show*. I must say I was disgusted, and not only by the fact that you would be pushing some ridiculous new age roasted red pepper alfredo sauce. That's for you and your dearly departed grandparents to hash out in heaven. What disgusted me more was the way the head chef kept yelling mangia every few seconds like one of those freaks who can't help from blurting out curse words in the middle of a conversation. Is that the only thing you could come up with to communicate to your customers that it's an Italian restaurant? If so, might I suggest you mangia shit and die.

Sincerely,
Tess Riccitelli
Goldwood Senior Community
New Haven, CT

* * *

In reference to your new "commercial":

Aren't you just hilarious? Every time you shout mangia in your new commercial it just cracks me up. Hey, maybe that can become your catchphrase like Emeril and his "bam." Why didn't you end the commercial with someone sleeping with the fishes, too? That would have been priceless! Now, when you're done with this letter go look up the word sarcastic in the dictionary, you fucking caricature.

Father Thomas Lucarelli
Saint Rocco's Church on the Cove

* * *

Dear Assholes,

First of all, I hope the lactose-intolerant picket your glorified diner en masse and rail against your new Americanized cream sauce. Second, I'm going to yell mangia to the maggots when they lower your head chef into the ground.

Oh-So-Sincerely,
Frederico Baggadonuts

* * *

To those of you not only capable of taking time out of your lives to write these types of letters but also of potentially coming up with other things to do with said time, I can only say: *Please* stop reading here. (Assuming you made it this far!)

CONCLUSION

In closing I would like to provide you with the transcript from a game show that was shelved for the very reason cited above. It was set to begin airing weekday nights on a major network when it was abruptly pulled. Denny Terio was pitched to host, but the pilot was shot with an unknown. What follows then is the transcript to the one and only episode of *A Wop-ping Good Time*, recorded exactly as the game was played by a "show runner" whose job it was to make note of every detail, from the major on down to the minor, should the show get picked up, which it did not.

Enjoy!

A WOP-PING GOOD TIME PILOT

LIGHTS UP

INT.: STUDIO
The set depicts a sprawling kitchen, with the host facing the audience and the contestants sitting on stools at what is passing for a counter.

HOST
Hello, and welcome! Are you ready to have a Wop-ping Good Time?

CUE Card Reading: Applause.
The audience applauds, as do our contestants.

HOST
You can do better than that! I said, are you ready to have a Wop-ping Good Time??

CUE Card Reading: Louder Applause or no free board games. The audience rages.

HOST
Let's get right to it then. Question number one: You're at a nice Italian restaurant and the waiter brings you your salad just a few minutes after you order the steak pizzaiolla. What do you do?

MAN
Depends on the dressing, I guess.

Audience laughs, and our contestant loves it. Host looks irritated. (Note: We may need to up his anger management classes to five a week.)

HOST
Are you finished?

MAN
Oh. Sorry. Well...I eat it, of course.

Buzzer sounds and the word CAVONE flashes on the screen for :20.

HOST
You push the salad to the center of the table with the hand that your watch is on and you don't eat it 'til after you have your entrée, funny guy.

Man seems surprised.

HOST (continuing)
Contestant #2. #2 is the last thing you are, baby.

(Note: Host behaves quite differently when contestant is a good-looking female. Inform casting directors.)

HOST (continuing)
A man a few pews ahead o' you smiles at you at church during Sunday mass. What do you do?

WOMAN
Smile back?

Buzzer sounds and the word PUTTANA flashes on the screen for :20.

HOST
Honey, it's church! But good for you. (beat) Now, contestant # 3. You're picking a girl up for your first date. You pull up to the house. What do you do next?

MAN
Well, if I want her old man or her brothers to kick the snot outta me I honk the horn.

Bell sounds and CUE Italian music. Scantily-clad show hostess brings over shot of Sambucca. (Note: Review tape and check with FCC. I think I see nipple.)

HOST
Contestant # 1, you got a tough act to follow there.

MAN
Hey, I got no problem with sloppy seconds.

Audience laughs, and our contestant, again, loves it. Host is positively irate. (Note: Go right ahead and book that extra anger management class, sans studio approval.)

HOST
I bet you don't, funny guy. Question: Your mother calls you at work and tells you to pick a prescription up for her on the way home. But you was lookin' at some possible OT. Whadda you do?

MAN
Looks like Ma's goin' without her meds!

Buzzer sounds and the word CAVONE flashes on the screen for :20.

Audience laughs weakly, while host seems incapable of restraint. He pulls something out from inside his sport coat. Review tape; it may be a cigar cutter.

HOST
Oh, is she? Your own mother? The woman who bore your sorry ass? Then you can do without a finger!

CUT to commercial.